WOOD TURNING

A CRAFTSMAN'S GUIDE

WOOD TURNING
A CRAFTSMAN'S GUIDE

MARK BAKER

THE GUILD OF MASTER CRAFTSMAN PUBLICATIONS

First published 2012 by
Guild of Master Craftsman Publications Ltd
Castle Place, 166 High Street, Lewes,
East Sussex BN7 1XU

ISBN 978-1-86108-849-9

Publisher Jonathan Bailey
Production Manager Jim Bulley
Managing Editor Gerrie Purcell
Senior Project Editor Virginia Brehaut
Copy Editor Tom Mugridge
Managing Art Editor Gilda Pacitti
Design Simon Goggin

All photographs by Aaron Shedlock except
on the following pages:
Alan Goodsell: 98, 108 and 116
Anthony Bailey: 2, 5, 6, 9, 10, 12, 19, 24 (top),
25 (bottom), 27, 28, 30, 35, (bottom right), 40, 57,
61, 65 (pic 21), 66, 73, 82, 85 (top left), 89 and 93
Nick Arnull: 11 (all)
Courtesy of Brimarc: 32 (top left)
Courtesy of Tormek: 32 (top right)

Illustrations by Robin Springett

Set in DIN
Color origination by GMC Reprographics
Printed and bound in China by Hing Yip Printing Co. Ltd

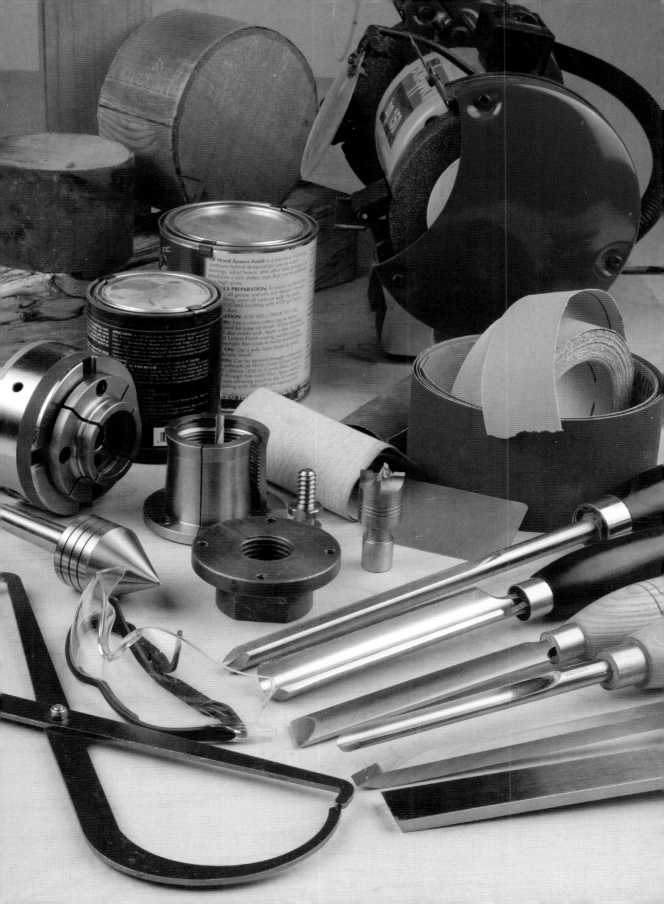

CONTENTS

INTRODUCTION

Wood turning is a fascinating and highly rewarding craft that allows you to explore your creative abilities and desires, while working with a wonderful natural material, in a way that no other type of woodworking can.

I started working with wood from a very early age and have been fascinated with it ever since. Each piece is different in its appearance, working and tactile qualities. I have yet to find another material that allows such a chance to explore and experiment in my quest to craft something of beauty.

Wood turning is one part of my journey in working with wood and it is a fascinating discipline that allows you to really explore your creative abilities. The use of the lathe opens up possibilities that will allow you to shape work in a way that is unique from all other woodworking disciplines. Wood turning also has an extensive, active, and vibrant community of people around the world.

When I started out on my journey in turning wood I met and read about many wonderful people who heavily influenced my development, and the techniques I use today are similar to those I learned at that time. I owe a great debt to Richard Raffan, Bert Marsh, Keith Rowley, John Jordan, Allan Batty, Ray Key, Chris Stott, John Hunnex, David Ellsworth, Tony Boase, Mike Darlow, and many more turners—too many to mention them all by name—who were always willing to share their time, experiences, and techniques and offer kind, encouraging words.

In the spirit of all the other turners who have shared their experiences and encouraged people like me to turn, I would like to share my own experiences with you. In this book I will show you the core techniques you need to get started as well as some helpful guidelines to remember and I hope you have as much fun with turning over the coming years as I continue to have.

WOODWORKING SAFETY

Woodworking is an inherently dangerous pastime and many safety precautions must be taken when using both hand- and power-tools. Always read the instructions supplied with your equipment, tools, and other accessories. Make sure that you use the safety devices supplied with your tools and use other personal protection equipment as necessary to minimize risk of harm to yourself. Always adhere to manufacturer's instructions. Always work within your limits and do not attempt a woodworking process that you are unsure of. I hope you enjoy your woodworking, but must stress that safety is the most important consideration.

WORKING WITH WOOD

Let's start by looking at wood. It is a treasured material and, as turners, we are fortunate in being able to use many varieties—we can choose wood according to its color, strengths, and working abilities. As your own experience develops you will find out which woods you prefer to work with and which types are best for a particular job.

There are many companies who supply wood to turners. It can be bought in the form of logs **1**, boards **2**, or precut pieces of a given shape, known as blanks. To start with it is easiest and most convenient to use blanks. They are available in various shapes and sizes and can be round **3** or square **4** depending on your requirements and to suit different types of turning. However, blanks are more costly—and when you progress and become more confident, you may, if space allows, look at buying planks or logs and cutting wood to the size you require.

TYPES OF WOOD

Wood is classified as either hardwood or softwood. Softwood usually comes from a tree that does not shed its leaves during winter—four examples are spruce, pine, yew, and larch. Softwood is often used in construction and is sometimes used when turning columns, spindles, and balusters **5**. Hardwood typically comes from a tree that sheds its leaves in winter. This type of tree is usually slower growing and the wood is usually harder and denser than softwood and used on a wider variety of projects. Hardwoods include oak, ash, maple, and walnut.

Good woods to use when learning to turn are close-grained dense woods such as maple, sycamore, and fruitwoods; these are used for turning projects such as spindles, bowls, and platters **6**.

SEASONING

Wood can be bought green and unseasoned, partly seasoned, air-dried or kiln-dried, and the moisture content will vary accordingly. How to season and dry wood, and how the wood moves and behaves during this process, are important issues but too in-depth to cover here in great detail. For the purposes of this book I will assume that you are using off-the-shelf, precut blanks. These can be used straight away with no fuss and are readily available in many retail outlets.

INTRODUCTION
TO THE LATHE

All wood turning requires the use of a lathe. Lathes come in various shapes and sizes to suit your budget and the size of your workshop. Lathes can be bench- or floor-mounted, but they all have similar key features.

ANATOMY OF A LATHE

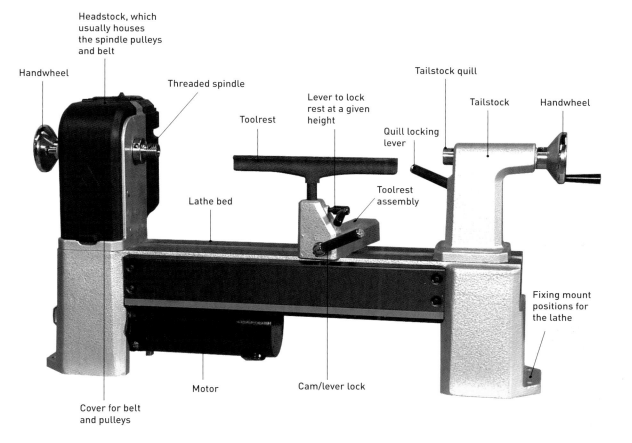

Headstock, which usually houses the spindle pulleys and belt

Handwheel

Threaded spindle

Toolrest

Lever to lock rest at a given height

Tailstock quill

Quill locking lever

Tailstock

Handwheel

Lathe bed

Toolrest assembly

Cover for belt and pulleys

Motor

Cam/lever lock

Fixing mount positions for the lathe

WORKING HEIGHT

Lathes from different manufacturers vary a little but their primary purpose is always to provide a stable platform on which to hold the wood. The lathe is used to make the wood rotate in a controlled manner while you are working on it.

You should be able to stand at the lathe and work at a comfortable height that does not cause you to hurt your back when turning. A quick way to find the position that is suitable for you is to stand at the headstock end of the lathe and bend your arm at 90° to the spindle (see picture right). The lathe should be at elbow height, give or take an inch or so. You can adjust it a little either way to suit your requirements, but this is a useful guide.

HEADSTOCK

The headstock is the housing for the main spindle shaft. The spindle has a precision-machined threaded section on it, which is used to fit a variety of items that enable you to hold and position the wood while it is turned **1**. The size of the spindle and the size of the threaded section vary from lathe to lathe. The most common sizes are ¾in x 16 tpi (teeth per inch), 1in x 8 tpi, 1¼in x 8 tpi and 33 x 3.5mm.

Most lathes also have a tapered hole, known as a Morse taper, in the end of the threaded spindle, and this too allows you to fit various accessories **2**, which we will look at in more detail later. Morse tapers come in a range of sizes numbered 0–7. The most common sizes found on wood turning lathes are: No.1, which is found on some of the smaller lathes; No.2, which is the most common; and No.3, which is used on a few of the largest lathes available **3**.

On the opposite end of the spindle, on the outer section of the headstock, the lathe often has a handwheel that allows you rotate the spindle by hand **4**. The size and shape of these vary but, and this is important, the lathe must be switched off before touching the handwheel.

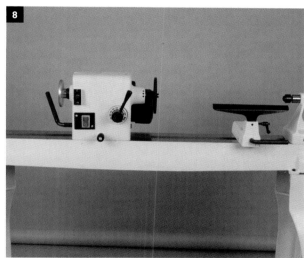

A lathe may also have an indexing system, which enables the spindle to be locked in any one of a given number of positions. There are usually 24 positions, but this may vary. The pin is placed in one of a series of holes that are usually found in the pulley nearest the outer section of the headstock . Indexing is great for certain drilling and cutting jobs.

Your lathe may have a fixed headstock, a swivel headstock, or a movable headstock. A fixed headstock is, as the name suggests, fixed in position and always has the spindle in line with the bed . A swivel headstock can be unlocked from the standard position in line with the lathe bed and rotated so the spindle can be moved to a different position. This can make access to the work easier for some projects . Left-handed turners may find the latter type of lathe easier to use than a standard fixed headstock model. It allows the headstock to be turned for a more comfortable position when faceplate turning. A movable headstock can be unlocked and slid to any position along the bed. This type might have a swivel facility too .

LATHE BED

The lathe bed usually compromises one or two round bars, or rectangular or T-shaped sections with flat tops. If the lathe bed has more than one bar or section, they will be parallel to each other and usually run the length of the lathe. Depending on the construction of the bed, the sections can be made from cast iron or fabricated steel. This provides a base for the toolrest assembly and tailstock, which are fitted to the bed and can be moved along it **1**.

TOOLREST ASSEMBLY

The toolrest assembly—sometimes known as a banjo—is a movable holder for the toolrest that can be securely clamped to the lathe bed by means of a cam-operated or threaded locking device. The toolrest is located in a machined hole that accepts the stem of the toolrest, and it can be raised, lowered, and swiveled to suit your needs by means of a locking mechanism. The toolrest itself can come in various lengths and is the support for the tools you use when cutting wood **2**.

TAILSTOCK

The tailstock unit slides up and down the lathe bed and can be locked in any position. The locking mechanism can be a bolt system underneath or, more commonly on modern lathes, a lever cam system. It is the housing for what is known as the tailstock quill. The quill can be wound forward and back with a handwheel, and, like the headstock, has a Morse taper hole in the end of it to accept various fittings. These fittings are used to centralize and support work **3**. This image shows the back face of the tailstock of this particular make of lathe, which, in this instance, has the lever-lock mechanism to secure the tailstock in position on the lathe bed.

MOTOR, PULLEYS, AND SPEED

Of course, the lathe cannot work unless there is some power to make the spindle go round. The motor is always located near the headstock—housed inside, behind, or under it . There is usually a stepped pulley wheel on the motor shaft . This has a sister pulley wheel, which is positioned in line with it on the headstock spindle. To transmit the power from the motor to the spindle, there is a pulley belt that can be shifted from one pulley position to another; each stepped pulley position corresponds to a specific speed . Many lathes have three to five speeds, ranging from somewhere around 300–400 rpm to a top speed of about 2000–3000 rpm, with various speeds in between 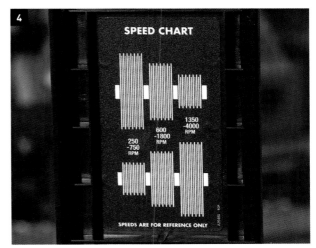. A good range of speeds is essential in order to turn a variety of projects, from small items up to larger capacity pieces. To facilitate the movement of the belt, the motor can be unlocked and raised via a lever-lock system: raise the motor to release tension off the belt and move it onto a new pulley. Once in position, the belt is shifted and the motor lowered to create tension in the belt; it is then locked back in position. This is known as manual speed changing. This must always be done with the lathe switched off. There are a couple of other ways to change the speed of the lathe. The first is called manual

SPEED CHART

250
-750
RPM

600
-1800
RPM

1350
-4000
RPM

SPEEDS ARE FOR REFERENCE ONLY

variable-speed, whereby a lever is pulled or pushed while the lathe is running to vary the speed—the pulley system changes shape to suit the speed selected.

The other method is known as electronic variable-speed. This requires you to twist a dial on the control unit, which also has an on/off switch and may have a spindle reversing switch too. This type is more commonly used in conjunction with at least two pulley sets so that you can alter the speed within a given range on each pulley position. This is very useful, as the lower speed range is ideal for big work and generates more torque, while the higher speed range is ideal for use on smaller diameter projects.

In addition, there is a type of variable-speed lathe that employs no pulleys at all—the speed is altered via an electronic system directly connected to the motor, which is in turn connected directly to the spindle by a universal link. Variable speed is a nice feature to have, but it is not essential. As you may have guessed, variable-speed lathes are more expensive than the manual speed-change type **5**.

CAPACITY OF THE LATHE

The capacity of the lathe is measured in two ways. The first is called the swing over the bed—this is the maximum diameter of work that can be mounted over the lathe bed. This is determined by the distance from the center of the spindle to the top of the lathe bed **6**. If the toolrest assembly is brought up close to the headstock, the swing capacity is reduced due to the bulk of the assembly **7**.

The other way of measuring capacity is known as between centers. To take this measurement, move the tailstock as far from the headstock as it will go and retract the quill. Fit a drive in the headstock and a center in the tailstock and measure the distance between the two. This is the distance between centers **8**. Drives and centers vary in size and capacity between them may be reduced. Many lathes are now sold with centers.

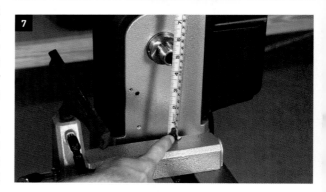

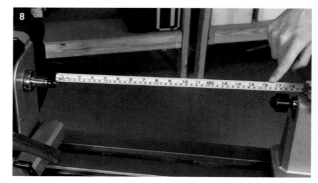

HOLDING THE WORK

Holding the work securely while turning is vital for safety reasons and to enable you to make controlled, clean cuts. Numerous accessories are available, and which ones you need depends on the specific nature of the work. However, in broad terms, turning can be broken down into two distinct types: faceplate turning and spindle turning.

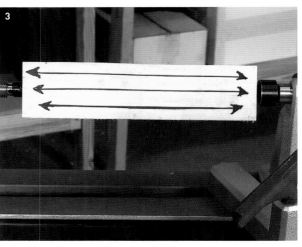

FACEPLATE TURNING

Faceplate turning typically has the grain running at 90° to the axis of the lathe when the headstock is in line with the tailstock. It facilitates the turning of bowls, dishes, and platters **1**. Most of the accessories used to hold work for this type of turning fit onto the headstock spindle **2**.

The term "faceplate turning" originates from a time when most bowls and platters were fixed to a faceplate but there are now many ways to hold work securely. The name is still valid, although a faceplate is only one of the items that can be used to hold the work. The key is holding the work securely and in a way that allows access to shape the wood safely.

SPINDLE TURNING

Spindle turning is also known as between-center turning, which refers to turning with the grain of the wood running parallel to the lathe bed **3**. This type of turning is usually used to produce items such as chair and stair spindles, balusters, support columns, goblets, boxes, spoons, pens, and so on. It typically employs accessories held on or in the headstock spindle in conjunction with support accessories that fit in the tailstock quill **4**.

HOLDING WORK FOR FACEPLATE TURNING

FACEPLATE

The faceplate is a machined piece of metal with a threaded female section at the back that fits onto the spindle of your lathe **1**. The top section is a flange, available in various widths, with countersunk holes through which screws are inserted into the work to firmly secure it. This method is best used on wood with a flat face to prevent any rocking of the chuck. The bigger the work, the wider the faceplate you will need to secure it and provide maximum stability. While the faceplate is usually affixed centrally to the work, there are occasions when it can be fixed off-center so you can turn items to a different shape. This is called off-center or multi-axis turning.

The faceplate is usually fixed on what will be the top section of the bowl. The screws should be long enough to provide a secure hold, but not so long that when the bowl is reversed (it is usually fitted to a scroll chuck for this process—see pages 22–3) you will not be able to turn away all the screw marks when hollowing out the inside **2**. When fitting work to the lathe, always check that it is secure before switching it on.

SCREW CHUCK

There are two types of screw chuck that you are likely to encounter. The first is similar to a faceplate but has a screw in the center of it. The flange of this type may also have screw holes in it **3**.

The second type is designed to fit the jaws of a scroll chuck. The screw fits in the center of the chuck and, when a workpiece is tightened onto the screw, the top rim of the jaws acts in the same way as the faceplate section and supports the work **4**.

In each case, a hole of the correct size is drilled into the wood—on what will be the top face of the work—and then the wood is screwed down onto the screw. This type of chucking is only to be used if the face of the wood is flat. If it is not, the wood will wobble and you will not get a secure hold. The larger the work, the wider or bigger the faceplate section needed to provide proper support. As with the faceplate, the screw chuck is usually fixed centrally to the work, but it can be used for off-center turning too.

CHUCKS

Chucks come in various shapes and sizes to suit different projects and types of lathe, but fundamentally, they screw onto the headstock spindle and have jaws that can be contracted or expanded to hold work and accessories. The most commonly used types are scroll or geared chucks, which can be opened and closed by using a type of key (the example shown here has a hexagonal key) **1**. The jaws can be contracted to clamp down onto a round tenon, also known as a spigot **2**. This is called compression mode. This holding method can be used for both faceplate and spindle work. It is important to ensure that the tenon is of a size that allows the jaws of your chuck to secure the work and gives as much jaw contact with the wood as possible. It is also vital that the tenon and recess are cut to the correct shape to suit the jaws. If you get the shape wrong, the hold is compromised **3** as shown in the drawings below. The tenon profile will typically be either parallel or dovetail in section. The larger the work, the larger the diameter of

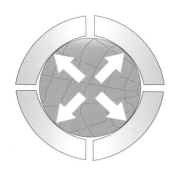

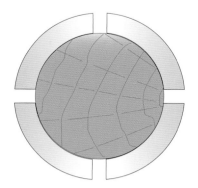

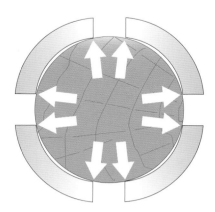

Tenon/spigot too small to have full contact with the jaw section and only gripped on the four sections indicated.

A correctly sized tenon for the jaw size used, offering maximum security of hold.

Tenon a little too big. The eight sections of the jaws indicated will bite into and mark the tenon gripped.

the jaws you will need to provide proper support. You can also hold spindle work with chucks. Here, the jaws are about to clamp onto a tenon cut on a piece of wood, which has the grain running parallel to the lathe bed **4**. Match the tenon shape to suit the jaws being used.

You can also expand the jaws of the chuck to hold in a recess **5**. This is called expansion mode. This method is commonly used for large, wide faceplate work such as platters and large bowls and, occasionally, on spindle work.

The first drawing below **6** shows the importance of cutting a hole of the correct size to ensure full contact with the jaws. The second drawing **7** shows how the recess or spigot must be the correct shape for the jaws you are using.

A little tip: it is worth making a note or drawing up a chart of the internal and external movement ranges of your sets of jaws. This means you won't have to keep cross-checking during your turning time, and you can set your measuring devices to a suitable size.

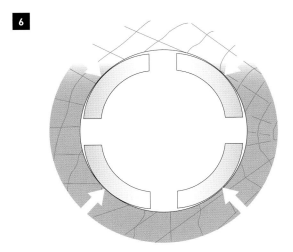

A recess that is too small for the jaws used – the piece of work is only gripped by a small fraction of each jaw.

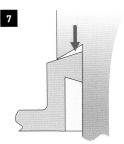

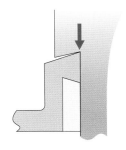

Dovetail jaws being used in expansion mode where the dovetail cut in the recess is the wrong shape for the jaws thus compromising the security of the wood.

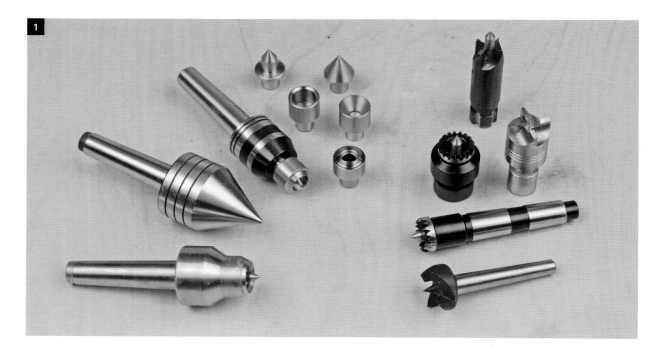

HOLDING WORK FOR SPINDLE TURNING

There are many accessories available for spindle turning, but they fall into two main categories: headstock and tailstock accessories **1**. We will look at both types in detail.

HEADSTOCK ACCESSORIES

Headstock accessories fit into the Morse taper or onto the threaded spindle on your lathe. As we saw in the faceplate turning section (see page 21), you can use a scroll chuck, which is versatile and allows you to insert various fitments to hold the work as well as gripping the wood directly **2**.

DRIVE SPURS

Drive spurs, also known as prong drives, vary in size and configuration **3**. They can be bought with Morse tapers to fit in the headstock spindle or to fit in a chuck. Typically they will have teeth that bite into the wood to drive it round. This image **4** shows a standard drive; the spurs or prongs are clearly visible. Drive spurs are named after their number of prongs—the one shown below is called a 4-prong drive because it has four cut prongs. Some drives have small teeth, which bite into the wood and there are other

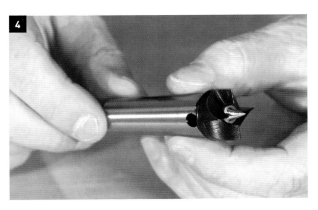

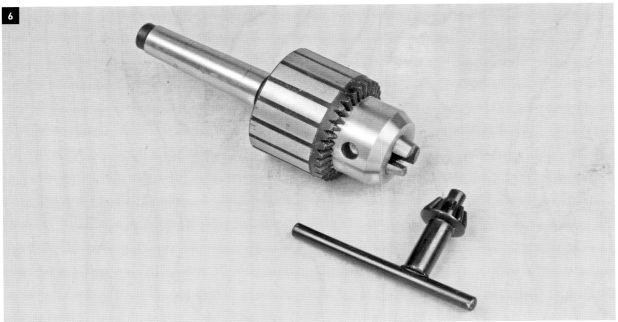

shapes available to help you to drive the work effectively. They have a Morse taper and fit into the spindle with the corresponding Morse taper hole. The two fit perfectly, but it is essential to keep the tapers clean. Some drives can be fitted directly into a chuck; as with this one **5**.

JACOBS CHUCK

The Jacobs chuck is similar to the chuck on an electric drill, but it has a Morse taper that fits into a slot in the headstock or tailstock **6**. It is usually key-operated, but keyless versions

are available. It can be used in the headstock to hold very small items such as finials, but it is more commonly used in the tailstock to hold drill bits, enabling you to drill a piece of work absolutely in line with the lathe bed.

No matter which driving or holding method you use in the headstock—and especially if you're using drive spurs—you are likely to need something at the tailstock end to support the work and allow the wood to run freely and in a secure and controlled manner. Safety is of paramount importance in all aspects of turning.

TAILSTOCK ACCESSORIES

The most commonly used tailstock accessories are revolving centers **1**. These support the wood but run on bearings to revolve freely, and typically push a small way into the end of the work to provide support. The basic revolving center is a pointed conical shape. Other profiles and sizes are available—which are used when you don't want a point to penetrate too far into the wood—or to support an odd shape as shown in pics one and two. Some revolving centers allow you to change the tip according to the project in hand—shown lower right in the image **2**.

To mount a spindle, start by marking the centers of the wood. Various tools and methods are available to help you find the centers of a piece of wood, but a pencil, finger, and straight edge can often work just as well. When you have marked the center positions at both ends, align the headstock end of

the wood, then the tailstock end, and bring up the tailstock so that the revolving center is almost touching. Lock the tailstock in position, use the handwheel to wind the revolving center into position, locate it, and turn the handwheel a little more to provide a bit of pressure. Lock it off with the quill locking lever. Take care not to apply too much pressure from the tailstock or you may cause the spindle to bend. With the toolrest clear, check the piece for security of hold.

You can hold large logs and spindle sections in this way to initially shape them prior to fitting them into a chuck for better access **3**. Here we are looking at holding the work; we will examine safety issues, toolrest positions, and the tools used to shape the work later on. Although they are mainly used in spindle turning, revolving centers can also be used to centralize and support bowl and platter work **4**.

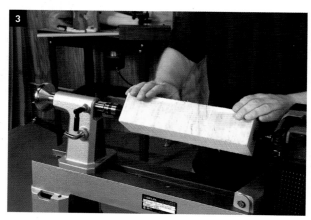

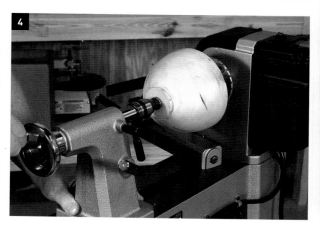

TOOLS AND EQUIPMENT

There is a vast array of tools available for you to buy. Many are variants of each other and are available in different sizes. This can be confusing when you are starting out, but to begin with you only need a few basic tools, as outlined on these pages.

ANATOMY OF A TOOL

Most turning tools are now made from High Speed Steel (HSS). There are different grades of steel, but M2 HSS is the most common; it gives a superb cutting edge when sharpened and lasts a reasonable amount of time.

I recommend seven basic tools to start off with. They are as follows: a bowl gouge, a spindle gouge, a parting tool, a beading and parting tool (these are thick and thin versions of each other), a spindle roughing gouge, a skew chisel, and a scraper or scrapers.

All turning tools, irrespective of type, have the same basic features: the cutting edge, which is typically at the top of the tool; a bevel, which is underneath the cutting edge; the blade of the tool; the tang, which is the section that is secured in the handle; and the handle itself, which comes in various lengths to suit the size of the tool.

In the case of gouges, the blade of the tool has a flute running about two-thirds of the way along it. The cutting edge that it produces has a bottom section and two sides. These sides are commonly known as wings. Depending on the shape of the cutting edge, the wings can be quite short or sometimes quite long.

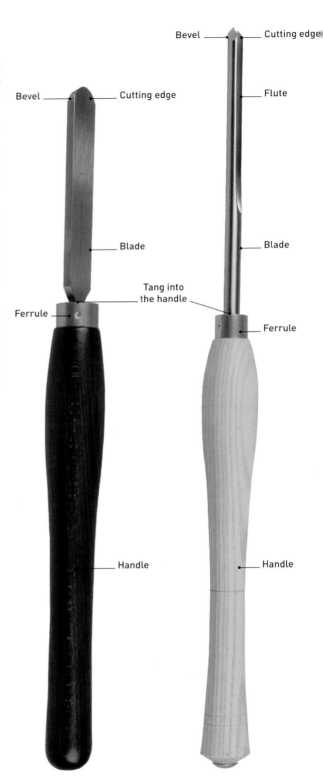

TOOLS FOR FACEPLATE TURNING

Faceplate turning typically requires a bowl gouge, parting tools, and scrapers. These should give you everything you need to shape and refine your project.

BOWL GOUGE

A bowl gouge is typically milled from a round bar, which has a deep flute running along about two-thirds of the blade toward the handle. The flute, depending on the make, can be a U shape, a V shape, or a parabolic curve. It is initially used for rough shaping, by removing lots of wood quickly, then to refine the curves on bowls and platters. A ⅜in (10mm) gouge is a good size to start with. There are various grinds that can be made on the end of the tool, and these grinds subtly affect how the tool can be used. The two most widely used grinds **1** are a fingernail or swept-back profile (left) or a standard grind (right). While the tool is known as a bowl gouge, its construction also allows it to be used on spindle work.

PARTING TOOL AND BEADING AND PARTING TOOL

The standard versions of the parting tool and the beading and parting tool are usually rectangular or square in section, although other shapes are available. They typically have two bevels at the front end that converge to create a cutting edge. They are effectively chisels, used to shear timber fibers

cleanly. The thinner ⅛–¼in (3–6mm) parting tools are ideal for making thin parting cuts and creating delicate fillets **2**. The wider ¼–½in (6–12mm) beading and parting tools are ideal for cutting larger tenons, spigots, fillets, and V cuts **3**.

A few specialized parting tools have flutes down only one cutting edge and are used to cleanly shear the fibers of the wood when parting off timber. If the flutes are deep enough, and are the right shape, they can be used to cut fine beads too.

SCRAPERS

Scrapers are usually flat, rectangular bars, which have various shaped sections on the end and are available in various widths. They are usually used to clean up and refine the work after it has been shaped with a gouge. A 1in (25mm) scraper with a rounded end is an excellent choice to start with but, depending on the work you undertake, you may need a square design or one with a raked end (rake means at an angle), and also a side-cut one for working boxes **4**. The larger the work, the greater the contact with the tool edge that is required to create a smooth curve or surface. If you use a ½in (12mm) scraper on a large bowl, you will create more ridges than you take out; if you use a large scraper with a large cutting area in contact with the work, you will smooth out the shape very easily.

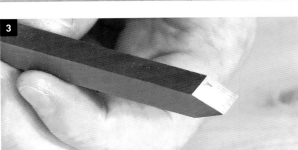

TOOLS FOR SPINDLE TURNING

The basic tools required for getting started with spindle work are a spindle roughing gouge, a spindle gouge, parting tools, skew chisels, and scrapers.

SPINDLE ROUGHING GOUGE

The spindle roughing gouge is usually made from a forged flat bar or, less commonly, a milled round bar . The photo shows forged tools. The flute—the channel down the center of the tool—is typically U-shaped, or very close to it. It is only to be used on spindle work in which the grain is parallel to the bed of the lathe. The tool is used between centers to smooth timber from square or log section down to round, and can be used to roughly shape the exterior of the work before you put in the detail with a spindle gouge. The large flute allows you to work on various sections of the cutting edge and its size allows for very quick removal of timber. Despite its size and shape, it can be used with surprising finesse when shaping long, sweeping curves. You must keep the toolrest as close to the work as possible when using this tool. Start with a ¾in or 1in (20mm or 25mm) tool, which is very versatile and will give you the flexibility to work on projects of many different sizes.

1

SPINDLE GOUGE

The spindle gouge is used for creating fine detail such as coves and beads, and for creating and refining shapes on spindle work. It is usually made from a milled round bar, but can be forged from a flat bar; the flute is shallow and typically semi-circular in shape. The profile is totally different to that of a bowl gouge, and, as with the spindle roughing gouge, the toolrest should be kept as close to the work as possible. A good size to start with is ⅜in (10mm) **2**.

SKEW CHISEL

The skew chisel is the woodturner's equivalent of a wood plane. When presented at a shear cutting angle, it peels the wood off, leaving a fine finish. It can also be used to roll beads and create incised V cuts. Skew chisels are typically oval or rectangular in section **3**. A ¾–1in (20–25mm) tool is a good starting size for beginners.

BEADING AND PARTING TOOL

As we saw on page 29, parting tools and beading and parting tools are great for spindle and bowl work. The tools can also be used to roll beads on spindle work.

SCRAPER

Scrapers **4** are hardly ever used on the outside of spindle work, but they can be used to clean up the inside of boxes, goblets, egg cups, and similar projects. By far the most common shape of scraper used on spindle work is one with a French curve, shown bottom left.

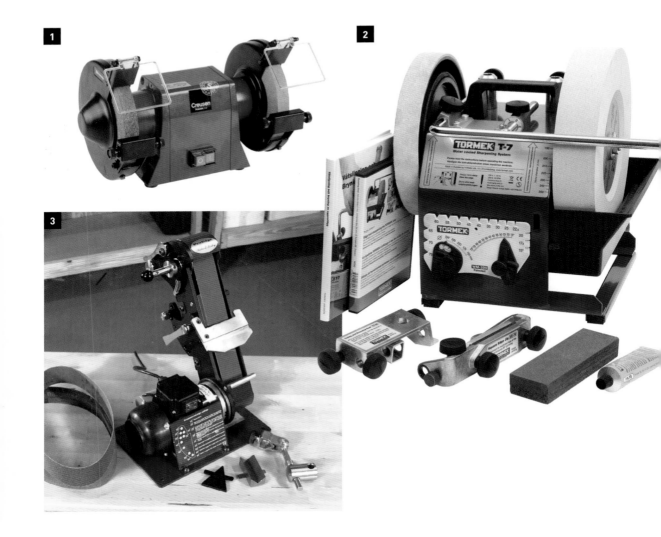

SHARPENING EQUIPMENT

Now you've bought your tools, you will need to keep them sharp. There are various pieces of equipment available to help you do this, including bench grinders **1**, water-cooled systems **2**, and belt-sharpening systems **3**. These all use different grades of abrasive wheels or belts to shape and sharpen the cutting edge of your tools.

The method that is most commonly used by turners is bench grinding. The other methods are good too, but bench grinders can be picked up for very little money and come fitted with two wheels—one coarse-grit wheel that is used to shape tools, and the other a fine grade used for sharpening the cutting edge. It must be said that the wheels supplied on cheaper grinders are often not really designed for turners. However, replacement wheels—usually aluminum oxide with a friable bond that breaks down to keep a fresh cutting surface in use—are available from wood turning suppliers. These companies may also supply grinders already fitted with such wheels. Shop around and ask some questions of fellow turners and the retailers before you part with your money to make sure you are getting what you need. Grinders usually come supplied with guards and a small rest. Make sure you fit and use the guards supplied. The rests vary in size. Ideally its size should allow you to fully support the tool during the sharpening or grinding process.

Before jigs came along, people often sharpened freehand just using a simple rest—and many, including myself, still use this method at times. For consistency and accuracy, jigs have been created by various manufacturers that all, by one method or another, allow you to accurately set up grinding angles and sharpen the tools easily, in a repeatable manner **4**.

Most tools can be sharpened on what is called a rise-and-fall-tilt table. The table can be adjusted to any angle required and provides a stable platform to place tools **5**.

Another method is to use a rocking arm, or fingernail jig; this is usually used for bowl and spindle gouges. This type of jig allows you to set a given bevel angle and to adjust how much the wings of the gouges are ground back **6**. No matter which system you use, make sure that you work at a comfortable height and in a position that allows you to see the sharpening taking place. Of course, wear eye protection when sharpening and make sure all the guards are in place. We will examine the process of sharpening your tools in more detail on pages 40–53.

HONES

Diamond, ceramic, and natural hones are available, but these are designed to create and maintain an edge, not to profile a tool **7**.

PERSONAL PROTECTIVE EQUIPMENT

Wood turning poses some risks to the turner. There are sharp tools, spinning wood, shavings, and chippings coming off the work, some at very high speed as it is being shaped and cut. Dust is also produced during the cutting stages and the final sanding stages. Certain finishes may contain chemicals which can also present a hazard when skin comes into contact with them or you inhale the vapor.

It is essential that you look after yourself and minimize the risks and dangers. There is plenty of equipment available that will help you to do this.

First, protect your eyes and face. As a minimum, you should use eye protection **1**, but a full-face shield **2** can further limit the risk from chippings and shavings. In addition, you must always make sure that all loose items of clothing are kept well away from the lathe—especially sleeves. Long hair should be tied back out of the way and items of jewelry should be removed when turning.

These precautions, however, do not eliminate the risk from dust. You can wear a mask or respirator-type filter system over the nose and mouth **3**; these come in various shapes and sizes and are also rated for use in different environments or with different materials and chemicals. They have ratings, so check that the one you buy is suitable for wood dust; you may also be able to find one that is able to deal with lacquer and finish vapor as well as wood dust. These can be disposable or may have replaceable filters. Powered respirators are becoming ever more affordable; and have a battery-operated filtering system and integral

full-face protection **4**. There are numerous types available, but they all operate in a similar way. Again, check the rating of the filter to make sure it is suitable for the projects you are working on.

All this will give you some degree of personal protection, but ideally dust and chippings also need to be removed from the environment. Numerous types of vacuum-type extraction systems allow you to have an extraction point close to the work, which will remove the bulk of the material produced **5**. It is best to deal with this as close to the source as possible, so there is less to worry about later on.

Ambient air extraction systems are also worth mentioning. These units are placed on the wall or suspended from the ceiling; they suck in the air from the workshop, filter out the dust particles, and pump the cleaner air back into the workshop, and can do so very effectively. Make sure it is sited so that it draws the dust away from, not past, the user **6**.

Many types of gloves are available to help minimize skin contact when handling finishes. Disposable ones are inexpensive and easy to find. Check that yours are suitable for use with finishes—the type shown here are vinyl. Using these on stationary work is fine, but be careful—if the gloves touch revolving work they can catch and become caught, which is a very dangerous situation **7**.

There is another issue, and that is one of adequate ventilation. Certain finishes have harmful vapors. Good, clean air flow is essential when using them and if in doubt use them outside to minimize your exposure to them.

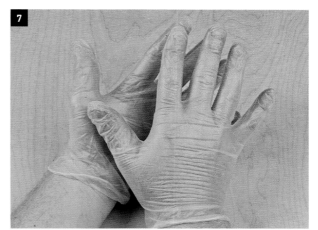

MEASURING AND MARKING EQUIPMENT

You will need to be able to measure and mark various types of work and there are several tools that will be of help to you **1**. Of course, a tape measure and a rule are essential, but calipers are also very useful. Calipers come in various sizes and, depending on their shape, enable you to measure internal and external dimensions, wall thickness, and so on. It is also worth noting that fingers can detect variations and changes where rulers and calipers do not, so a combination of approaches with measuring and marking is necessary to obtain the best results. But you must never check the work in this way when the lathe is revolving.

A pencil is vital in the workshop, as it allows you to make marks that can be easily removed later. Markers are useful but be careful where and when you use them. The marks are harder to remove and the ink can sometimes bleed into the wood. You may also find it useful to have a center-finder device **2**—this can save a lot of fiddling around.

ABRASIVES

Nearly all work is sanded, or abraded. Sandpaper gave us the word "sanding," but it has long been superseded by superior abrasives that cut more cleanly with less heat build-up, last longer, and are generally more flexible. These are the qualities of a good abrasive for the turner.

Abrasives are used to refine the surface of the work prior to the application of a final finish. Aim to have a good range of abrasives, from 100-grit, which is coarse, down to 400-grit, which is classed as a fine grit grade. Abrasives come in various types: aluminum oxide, diamond, silicone carbide, and so on. Each is designed for use on specific materials. The abrasive most commonly used by turners is aluminum oxide, which is bonded to a backing that can be resin-bonded, cloth, or a form of paper. You can buy abrasives as precut sheets or as rolls, or parts of rolls in various widths **3**.

Turners generally use two types of sanding technique. The first is hand sanding, in which the abrasive is held in the hand against the rotating or stationary work and traverses

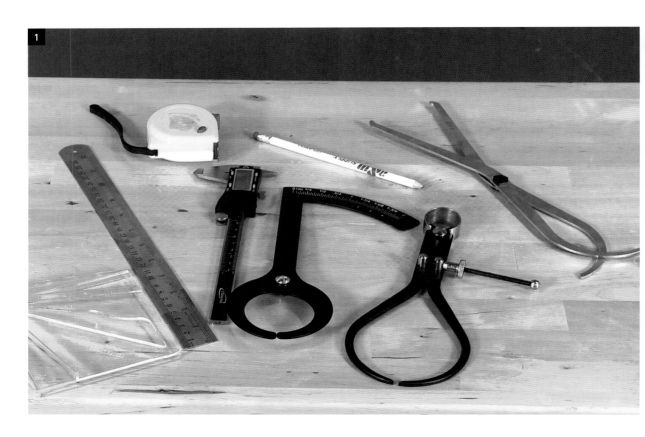

the surface to remove blemishes. The other is power sanding. For power sanding, you need an arbor with a hook-and-loop face onto which the abrasive is fixed, and a method of driving it, usually a drill. Revolving arbors are available in sizes ranging from ½in to 6in (12mm to 150mm) diameter; the most commonly used are 2in (50mm) and 3in (75mm) diameter. When the abrasive is fitted, the arbor is fitted to the drill and traversed across the surface of the revolving work with the drill running. The best results are achieved by having the arbor running in contra-rotation to the work on the lathe. This method of sanding is devilishly quick, and only a very light touch is required to prevent unwanted furrows from appearing.

Another alternative to power sanding is to use a passive or inertia sander. This comprises an arbor mounted in a bearing housing, which in turn is attached to a handle. The arbor is fitted with an abrasive and offered up to the spinning work; the rotational speed of the lathe spins the arbor.

Abrasives for this purpose have a loop backing and can either be bought precut to size, or in rolls to cut yourself. The abrasives stick on and can be removed when you have finished **4**. This is similar to using an orbital sander.

SANDING TIPS

No matter which sanding method you use, you should start with the coarsest grade you have to in order to remove any marks and blemishes left from the turning. When all the blemishes are removed, move on to the next grit grade, then work down through the grits. For example, if you started at 100-grit, you would then move on to 120-grit. Each subsequent grit removes the scratches left from the previous grit, and you work down until the scratches are so small and fine that you can't see them. So, after 120-grit, you move to 180-grit, then 240, 320, and so on until you achieve the finish you want. Sanding to 400-grit is usually more than enough for the work you will encounter when starting out.

FINISHES

Finishes are applied to seal, protect, and enhance the appearance of wood to bring out its full potential. Go to any hardware store and you will see a bewildering range of finishes to choose from **1**. It is important that you choose an appropriate finish for your particular project. Consider whether or not the item will to come into contact with food; whether the piece is purely decorative; whether it will be handled by people very often; whether it will it be used often; and whether it needs to be cleaned. If it does, the finish needs to be water-resistant or waterproof. Then ask yourself if the item will get stained when it is used. Salad bowls, for example, may have items such as beetroot placed in them, which can stain wood badly. This type of quick mental checklist will help you pick the correct finish. Finishes can be broken down into three main groups, outlined below.

PENETRATIVE FINISHES

Penetrative finishes such as oils penetrate the wood, seal it, and, depending on the type, form a superb protective barrier against marking, staining, and water damage. They can be used to create a matt, satin, or high-gloss luster. There are numerous types of finishing oil on the market but they are well worth exploring. Penetrative finishes are some of the easiest to work with when you are starting out **2**. They are easy to apply and use.

SURFACE FINISHES

Surface finishes such as sanding sealers, lacquers, and varnishes, can be wiped, brushed, or sprayed on, depending on the job. Sanding sealer is used as a base coat that seals the wood prior to sanding, or can be applied after sanding to form a protective base coat over which you can apply oil, lacquer, varnish, or wax **3**. Many of these form a hard protective surface when dry and, depending on the type used, can be durable and resistant to heat, scratches, and moisture. They are easy to use and are available in matt, satin, eggshell, and gloss lusters. When you're working on items with a lot of detail, take care not to allow build-up in detailed areas such as recesses and fillets.

SEMI-PENETRATIVE FINISHES

Semi-penetrative finishes such as wax can, depending on the type, be applied over existing finishes or to bare wood to create a surface luster that is easy to maintain **4**. Again, depending on the type used, they can offer a good degree of protection against marking during everyday use, touching, and wear and tear.

As you progress and experiment with your use of finishes, you will find your own favorite types and mixes of finishes that suit your work, and ways in which you can manipulate them to create a particular effect. Be patient: develop your skills on the basic finishes first and progress from there.

FINISH CONSIDERATIONS
Contact with food
Handling frequency
Utilization frequency
Possibility of cleaning
Possibility of stains

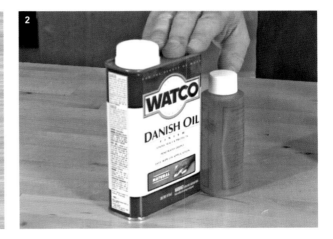

TECHNIQUE 1
SHARPENING YOUR TOOLS

Correctly ground and sharpened tools are easier to use, require less force in use and are the only way you can ensure as clean a cut as possible on the item being turned. There are a number of ways to grind and sharpen tools; the best way is the one that you are most comfortable with using.

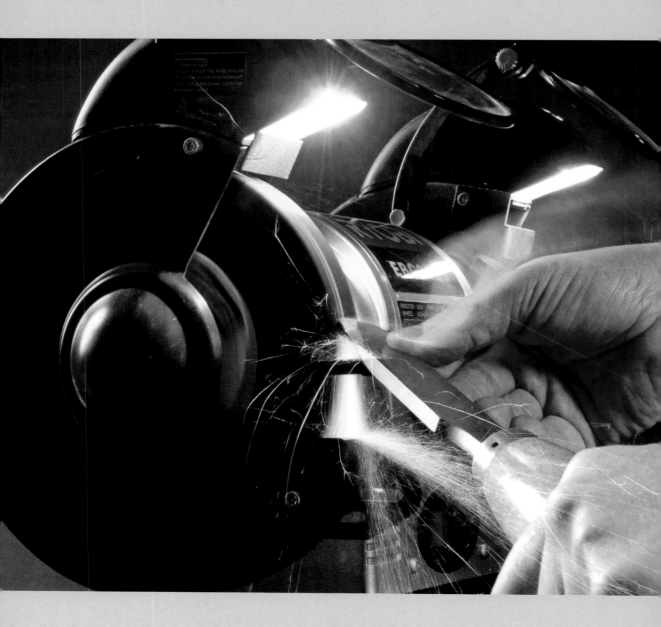

USING A BENCH GRINDER

There are usually two stages to creating a sharp edge. The first stage is to grind the tools to the shape and then create the bevel angle needed. The shape of the grind and the bevel angle are dictated by the type of tool, how the tool is ultimately used, and where it has to reach to cut the work. Grinding is undertaken using a coarse-grit wheel on a wet or dry grinder and/or belt on a linisher/belt-type system. This process is only undertaken when you need to reshape a tool edge or bevel or repair a damaged edge.

The second stage is to refine the cutting edge and this is done by using finer-grit abrasives to ensure the cutting edge is kept at its best. Before you start sharpening, make sure you are wearing eye protection or face protection **1** and that all the guards are in place. Make sure the rest is not too far from the wheel or belt, but of course it mustn't touch it. The rest must be able to support the tool properly without there being too much of an overhang between the rest and the wheel. The rest must be set at a height that allows the tool to be ground/sharpened in the top section of the wheel above the centerline **2**.

Make sure the wheel is nice and clean; clogged wheels do not cut, they just generate unnecessary heat. If your wheel is clogged, use the manufacturer's recommended cleaning method—in the case of bench grinder wheels it will be a devil stone, star wheel, or diamond matrix **3**. Use a light touch when sharpening; not much pressure is needed. Too much pressure or using a clogged wheel will generate heat and can blue the steel **4**.

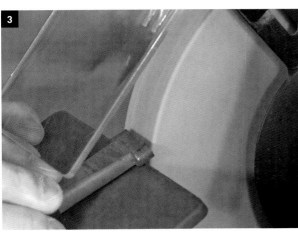

PARTING TOOLS AND BEADING TOOLS

Parting tools and beading and parting tools are variants of each other and come in various sizes and shapes. The standard forms are the easiest types of tool to sharpen. Set the toolrest to the required angle for the parting tool; the inclusive angle is typically anything between 30° and 45°. It is the intersecting line between the two identically shaped and ground faces that creates the cutting edge.

Parting and beading tools can be sharpened using a rise and fall table. First, with the grinder switched off, place the tool on the table and adjust the angle of the platform until the bevel being sharpened is perfectly aligned with the wheel, or is at the angle you require **1**. When you have the required angle, switch on the grinder and, holding the blade of the tool against the rest, gently push the tool forward up the rest until the cutting edge touches and is square on to the revolving grinding wheel. Maintain light pressure keeping contact with the wheel. It should only take a second or two to achieve a clean, sharpened face **2**.

Remove the tool and check the results. If you are satisfied, turn it over and repeat the process on the opposite side. Move the tool from side to side if necessary. Remember that the actual cutting edge is the flat point that is created where the two ground faces intersect **3**. Check the cutting edge regularly to make sure it is free of any nicks or flat spots.

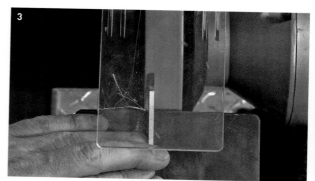

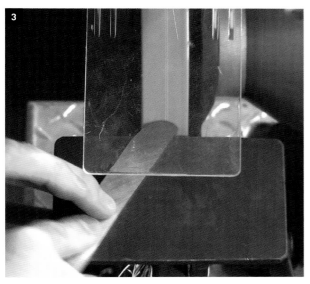

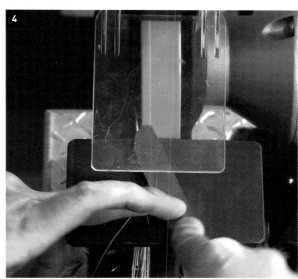

SCRAPERS

As we've seen, scrapers come in all sorts of shapes and sizes (see page 29). For your first scraper, I advocated purchasing a round-nosed scraper. This can be converted into what is called a French curved-edge scraper **1**, in which the cutting edge is ground a little farther down the side of the tool, making it much more versatile.

Sharpening this tool is similar to sharpening the curved-edge skew (see page 45). For the scraper, you need to create a bevel on only one side of the tool. First, set your grinder toolrest to the correct angle. This should be somewhere between 45° and 80°—to start with, try one at about 60° and see how you get on. Next, present the scraper at an angle to the grinding wheel. Push the scraper onto the wheel and sweep it around with your fingers, pressing the tool onto the rest and applying light pressure to the edge on the wheel **2** until the full scraping edge has been sharpened **3**. The edge is the intersecting line between the flat top of the scraper and the ground bevel **4**.

SKEW CHISELS

The standard skew chisel is another easy tool to sharpen. You need to grind a face on both sides of the tool to create an angled edge with a toe (the longest point) and a heel (the lowest section for the cutting edge). The sharpened edge is at an inclusive angle of 25–35°, and—when the blade is viewed from the flat side—it has a canted rake edge of about 25° **1**.

To sharpen a skew chisel, set your toolrest to the correct angle, switch on the machine, and grind one side **2**, moving the tool from side to side to make sure the whole edge is sharpened and you are using the whole face of the wheel. When you're happy with the results **3**, flip the tool over and grind the other side **4**.

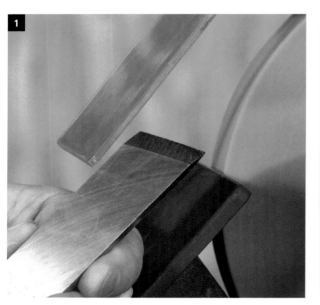

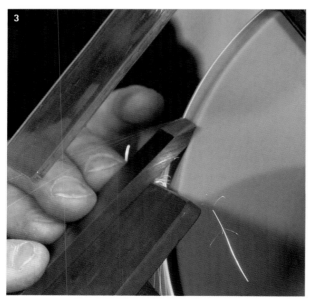

CURVED-EDGE SKEW CHISELS

Skew chisels can also be sharpened to create a curved edge **1**. Some claim this is a little easier to use than the standard grind. This profile is fairly easy to make—all you have to do is introduce a swinging action to the grind to create the curve. Again, set the toolrest angle and switch on the grinder. Start with either the long or short point of the cutting edge **2** and arc the edge on the wheel to create the required curve **3**. You will find that the arcing motion involved means you are likely using the whole surface of the wheel to shape/sharpen the cutting edge. As with the standard grind, when you're happy with one side, flip the tool over to grind the other face **4**.

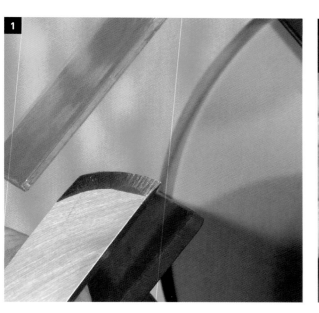

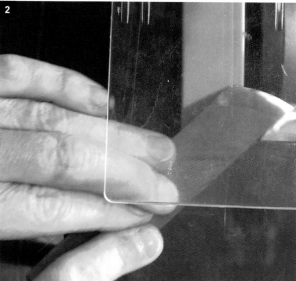

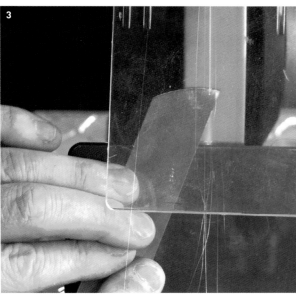

SPINDLE ROUGHING GOUGE

Of all the gouges, the spindle roughing gouge is the easiest to sharpen. First, set the rest to the required angle—between 35° and 60° is the norm. A 45° angle will serve you well to begin with. The cutting edge is the intersecting line between the inner flute profile and the ground bevel **1**.

Start anywhere you like on the cutting edge—find the position that is comfortable for you. Gently push the tool into the grinding wheel until it touches the wheel **2**. Keep the cutting tool square to the wheel and rotate the tool axis to grind the bevel **3** equally across all of the tool cutting edge **4**. The tool is usually ground square across, but the wings being ground back just a little is fine too. Keep rolling the tool from side to side until you have the whole edge sharpened **5**.

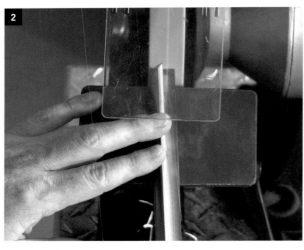

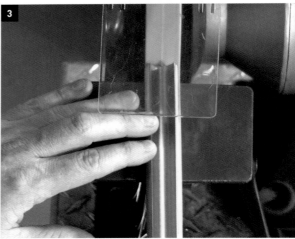

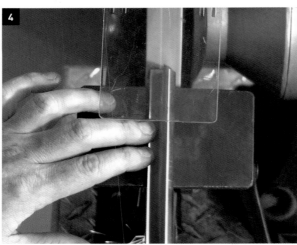

SPINDLE GOUGE

The spindle gouge is typically ground so the cutting edge is a swept-back profile often called a fingernail profile **1**. The typical front-end bevel angle is between 30° and 45° and the cutting edge is typically extended along the flute, about ⅜in (10mm) or so. This grind can be achieved in three ways, two by hand sharpening and one using a jig.

It's easy to create the swept-back form on a standard-grind spindle gouge. First, take the spindle gouge **2** and lay the tool flute down onto the wheel. Support the blade on the back edge of the rest **3**. The angle at which you present the tool to the wheel determines the length of the swept-back profile **4**. Now, with the profile shape made, let's look at sharpening it.

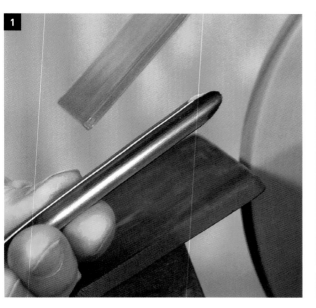

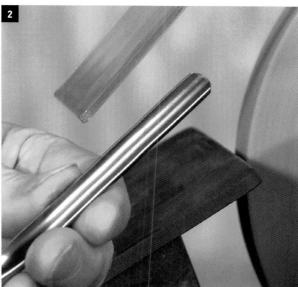

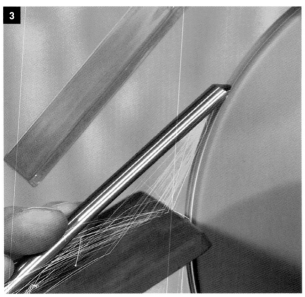

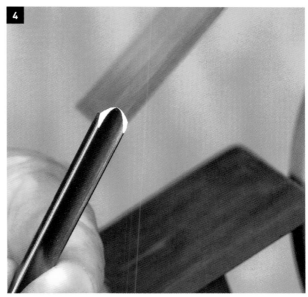

FREEHAND SHARPENING METHOD 1

Set the rest to the bevel angle required and position the tool on the back edge of the rest with the flute pointing at either the 3 o'clock or 9 o'clock position **1**. Rotate the blade while raising and lowering it on the wheel **2** **3** until you reach the opposite side of the flute. You will see that the flute points almost vertically when it is at the lowest part of the rise-and-fall movement; this is the point at which the front-end bevel is created. Carry on with this raising, lowering, and rotating process until you achieve the shape and edge you require **4**. You can see that the cutting edge curls back. This method is a little tricky at first but is worth knowing and doesn't require any extra equipment—just practice! **5**

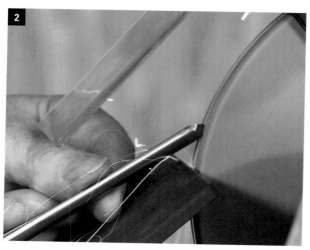

FREEHAND SHARPENING METHOD 2

Position the tool flat on the rest with the handle over to either the left or right, whichever is most comfortable. The images below show the blade over to the left; note that the flute is pointing to the 10 o'clock position **1**. Arc the tool handle to the right **2**, rotating the blade as you go **3**. Take it slowly and maintain the swinging motion while rotating the handle **4**. When the tool reaches the end of its travel, the flute points to approximately the 2 o'clock position **5**. Repeat the process until you have the required profile. The length to which the wings are ground back is up to you, but around ½in (12mm) is a good place to start.

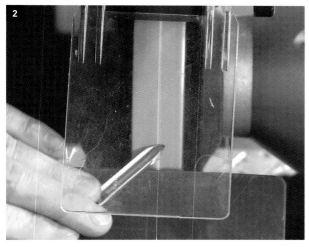

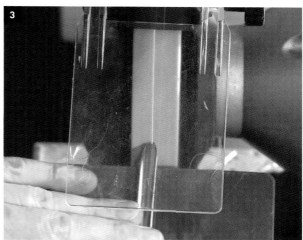

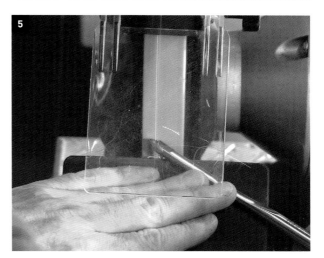

JIG METHOD

Freehand sharpening of the swept-back grind is not easy to master, and this is where a sharpening jig comes in very handy. Jigs are available that are specifically designed for sharpening swept-back grinds on bowl gouges and spindle gouges but, depending on type, can also be used to sharpen some scrapers, skews and parting tools. They consist of a clamp to hold the tool and an adjustable arm that enables you to modify the type of swept-back profile you require **1**. The jig will follow a given course as you move it around a predetermined arc or sweep, which twists the tool at the same time. This type of jig comes in many different forms, but they all perform a similar function. There are three settings you need to make. First, you set the angle of the arm that connects to the tool-holding clamp. This sets the angle of the bevel you are grinding—most jigs come with a measuring device to help you work out this angle. Next, you set the distance by which the tool will protrude from the clamping device, and the distance of the blade tip from the grinding unit. When

these parameters are set the jig will guide you as the tool arcs across the grinding wheel **2**. When you find the precise grind you like best, you can make a note of the settings and the projection of the gouge so you can repeat it again at a later date. Use the edge of your sharpening bench, or make a small jig, to mark how far each tool protrudes from the tool clamp. You can accurately replicate each bevel in this way. When you have set the angle required and the projection of the blade, you can begin sharpening. Start with the jig

off to the left or the right **3**. Apply pressure to the holder to maintain contact with the wheel. Keeping the pivot arm in the holder, swing the arm to the other side of the wheel in small stages **4** so the cutting edge is sharpened along the whole edge as you go **5**. Swing the unit back and forth as necessary to create the edge and profile required **6**. Do not use too much pressure. When this process is viewed from the top you can see how the process starts off to one side **7**. Then the arm is swung over to the opposite side **8**.

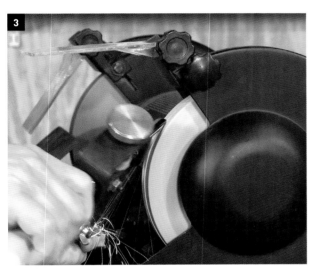

BOWL GOUGE

Two grinds are usually used in conjunction with bowl gouges **1**. Most bowl gouges are supplied with the standard grind (right-hand gouge), in which the wings are ground back very slightly. But a swept-back profile—also called a fingernail profile (left-hand gouge)—is probably the most commonly used grind because it gives the tool a larger cutting edge than the standard grind. The swept-back profile also gives the cutting edge easier access to tighter areas of the work. The shape of the gouge means this profile, although created in a similar way, looks slightly different from that on spindle gouge.

STANDARD GRIND

The sharpening method for this grind is very similar to the spindle roughing gouge (see page 46). To create the standard grind, set the position of the toolrest to the required angle—between 80° and 45° is a good angle to start with. Position the tool flat on the rest with the tool flute pointing directly to the right or left, i.e. at either the 3 o'clock or 9 o'clock position. Gently push the tool onto the grinding wheel **2** and rotate it **3**, keeping the tool centered on the wheel face **4** until the flute points to the opposite position **5**. Repeat this rolling from one side to the other until the edge is formed and sharp. You should also apply a very slight swing on the tool, to pull the wings back just off square by about 5°–10° **6**.

SWEPT-BACK PROFILE

The swept-back profile on a bowl gouge can be created using the same techniques as we used for the spindle gouge (see pages 47–50): Freehand method 1, rise and fall **7**; Freehand method 2, the swinging and rolling motion **8**; or the Jig method **9** **10**.

HONING

Honing is a method for maintaining the edge on your tools, rather than sharpening them. Simply lay the hone on the side of the tool, touching the heel of the bevel. Move it round **11** until the hone is in full contact with the heel of the bevel and the cutting edge **12**. Use a circular motion, maintaining full bevel contact all of the time, until you have honed all of the cutting edge. Repeat the process on the other side.

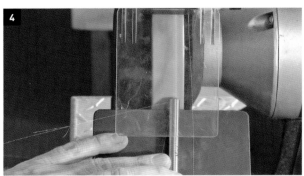

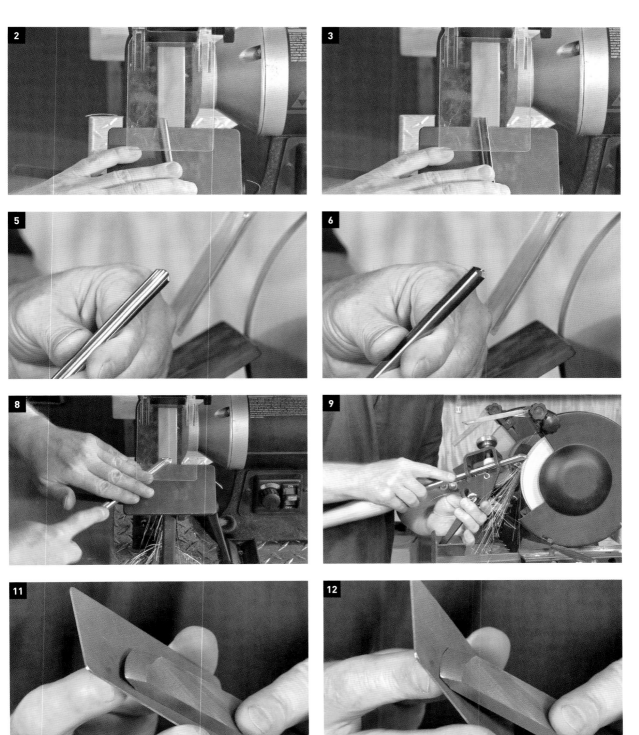

TEN RULES FOR TURNING

The guidelines on these pages are fundamental to good working practice and control of your tools. Before you start turning, you must be aware of the risks involved: items of work spinning at great speed, materials that may have naturally occurring flaws, sharp tools, and powerful equipment are just a few of the potential hazards. But it takes just a few sensible precautions and checks to minimize the danger.

RULE ONE

When mounting work on the lathe, double check that the work is held securely and everything is locked in place before switching on the lathe **1**.

RULE TWO

Before switching on the lathe, check that you have selected an appropriate lathe speed to suit the size, weight, length, and condition of the work being turned **2**.

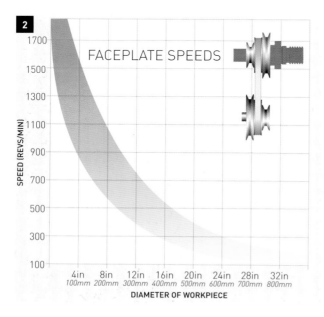

FACEPLATE SPEEDS

SPEED (REVS/MIN)

1700
1500
1300
1100
900
700
500
300
100

4in / 100mm 8in / 200mm 12in / 300mm 16in / 400mm 20in / 500mm 24in / 600mm 28in / 700mm 32in / 800mm

DIAMETER OF WORKPIECE

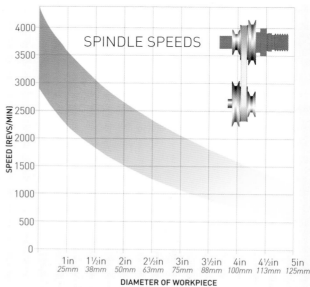

SPINDLE SPEEDS

SPEED (REVS/MIN)

4000
3500
3000
2500
2000
1500
1000
500
0

1in / 25mm 1½in / 38mm 2in / 50mm 2½in / 63mm 3in / 75mm 3½in / 88mm 4in / 100mm 4½in / 113mm 5in / 125mm

DIAMETER OF WORKPIECE

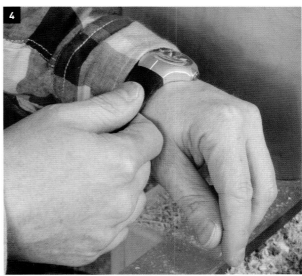

RULE THREE

Before starting the lathe, rotate the work by hand to make sure the toolrest—which needs to be as close as is practicable—is clear of the spinning work .

RULE FOUR

Make sure you are not wearing loose sleeves or items of clothing or jewelry that could get caught in the work. Tie long hair back out of the way ■.

RULE FIVE

The cutting tool should always be kept in contact with the toolrest before starting the cut and then remain in contact throughout ■.

RULE SIX

When using gouges, always have the flute pointing in the direction of the cut ■.

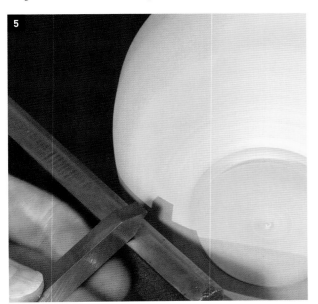

RULE SEVEN

Stop the lathe when moving the toolrest to a new position, or if you need to adjust its height **7**.

RULE EIGHT

For maximum control and to obtain the best finish, bevel-rubbing tools such as gouges, parting tools, and skew chisels should have the bevel rubbing against the work, so they cut the wood effectively **8**.

RULE NINE

Scrapers should be placed flat on the toolrest and used in trailing mode, i.e. with the handle higher than the cutting edge. This minimizes the risk of a catch **9**.

RULE TEN

Try to cut the wood downhill, or with the grain. This will mean there is always a longer fiber behind the one that is being cut, providing support and minimizing the likelihood of tearout **10**.

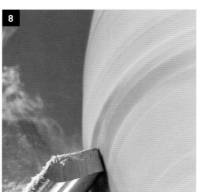

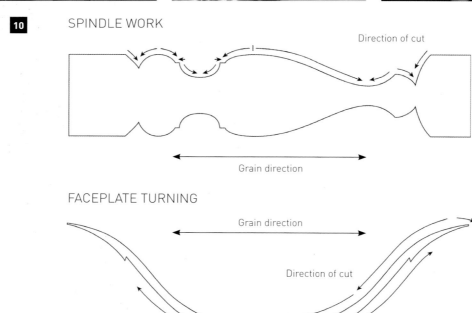

SPINDLE WORK

Direction of cut

Grain direction

FACEPLATE TURNING

Grain direction

Direction of cut

TECHNIQUE 3
CORRECT WORKING POSITION

When working at the lathe you must always stand in a position that is comfortable and enables you to move around easily. If you don't, your safety and tool control will be compromised. Similarly, tools must be held in a comfortable position that allows you to present the cutting edges to the work in the correct manner.

STANDING FOR FACEPLATE TURNING

Let's look at how we stand at the lathe when faceplate turning. Your body should be facing the lathe between the 10 o'clock and 12 o'clock positions in relation to the bed. Position your left foot at about the 11 o'clock position in relation to your body. Your feet should be just over hip width apart, with your right foot in line with or slightly back from your left foot, and pointing at roughly the 2 o'clock position **1**.

Your right hand will hold the handle of the tool low towards the hip, close to the body **2**. (If you are left-handed, hold the tool with your left hand and alter the position of your feet to stand in a way that allows you to access the work as easily as possible in the manner described.) Keeping your right hand and the tool handle near to your body whenever possible gives you more control and better tool support, and means that only subtle shifts in your body position are required to adjust the position of the tool **3**. The right hand is used to raise, lower, and rotate the handle as necessary to adjust the cutting position.

The left hand holds the blade of the tool with either an underhand **4** or overhand **5** grip (whichever is most comfortable and controllable for you), provides downward pressure to keep the blade in contact with the rest at all times, and moves the blade along the rest, allowing for micro adjustments of the cutting positions. The body and hands work in sync with each other to provide movement, control, and optimum support when cutting and moving the tool **6**. However, depending on the shape of the work being turned, be prepared to raise the right hand upward and away from the body in order to cut the inside of bowls and similar shapes—unless you have a swiveling headstock, this will mean you are working over the bars of the lathe bed.

In this image **7**, taken from above, you can see me cutting the outside of a bowl. My center of balance shifts from my right to my left foot as I work around the bowl, and the tool is supported on the body during the cut on the outside of the bowl.

If you follow these guidelines—making your own adjustments until you are most comfortable—you should be able to move your body in a flowing fluid movement while cutting the work in a controlled manner. Being comfortable when turning is vital but feel free to adjust the basic starting position to suit your own needs.

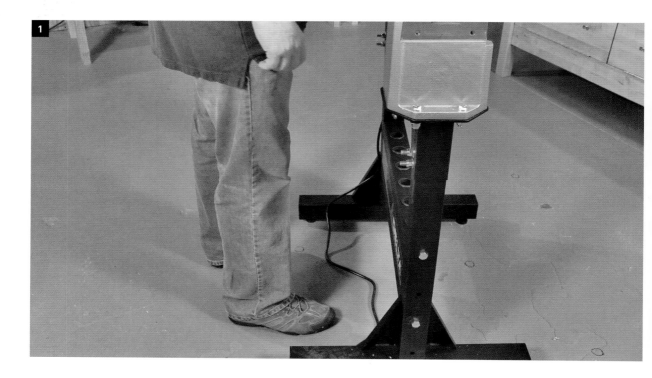

1

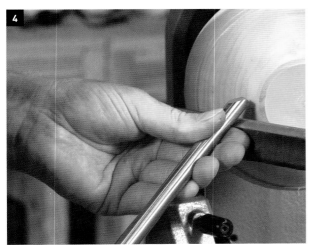

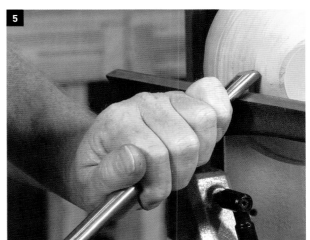

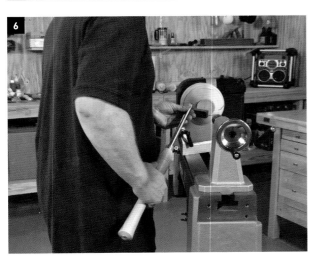

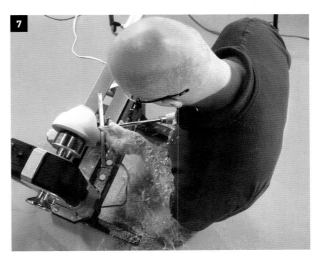

STANDING FOR SPINDLE TURNING

To describe the standing position for spindle turning, I am again going to assume you are right-handed. If you are not, reverse the positions of the feet and hands as necessary. If the lathe or bench feet are in the way, place your foot on the far side of them to achieve a more comfortable position. Stand facing the lathe with your legs slightly apart and point your left foot at the 11 o'clock position and slightly forward of the right foot, which should point toward the 2–3 o'clock position. Your feet should be about 2ft (60cm) apart and you should be able to shift your balance to either foot and adjust your body position without shuffling along the work **1**.

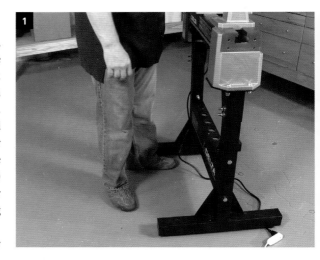

Your right hand will hold the handle of the tool low toward the hip, close to the body. As with faceplate turning, this gives you maximum tool control. The right hand is used to raise, lower, and rotate the handle as necessary to adjust the cutting position of the tool **2**.

As before, the left hand holds the blade of the tool with either an underhand or overhand grip, provides downward pressure to keep the blade of the tool in contact with the rest at all times, and moves the blade along the rest **3**.

By adopting a stance similar to this one you will be able to turn your body comfortably and move along the work as required without falling over or feeling awkward.

SAFETY

That's the stances covered, but remember—before starting any cut, run through the safety checks: is the work secure, eye and/or face protection, clothing, the rest position in relation to the work, lathe speed, and so on. Only when you are sure you are safe should you turn on the lathe and start cutting.

TECHNIQUE 4
USING SPINDLE ROUGHING GOUGES

The spindle roughing gouge has a wide, deep flute and a cutting edge, and is used with the bevel rubbing. It should only be used on spindle grain oriented wood—objects such as chair and table legs, goblets, and end-grain boxes. If you follow the guidelines on these pages you will gain maximum control over the tool and the cleanest cuts when using it.

GENERAL GUIDELINES

The spindle roughing gouge is not designed for faceplate work, where the grain runs at 90° to the axis of the lathe bed. Also, the blade or tang is not strong enough to cope with the cutting forces involved if it is presented with a large overhang on the rest. It is best to have the rest just under the centerline position of the spindle.

There should be enough downward pressure on the tool to keep the blade in contact with the rest but still allow it to be moved as required. The work should be secure and you must check that the work rotates clearly without fouling the rest—which should be close to the work and parallel to it.

Support the blade on the rest and use either the overhand or underhand grip to stabilize the tool on the rest. The overhand grip is more powerful, but the underhand grip allows for easier manipulation of the tool during the cut. If you use the overhand grip you will also encounter shavings coming down the flute during the cut; these can sting the hand as they pass over it, especially with dry splintery wood **1**.

STANDARD ROUGHING DOWN CUT

The bevel must always be supported by the wood, so never begin a cut from the end of the work, but start just away from

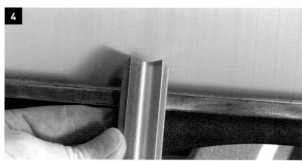

one end and cut towards it. Using successive cuts, move the starting point of the cut back toward the center section. Keep cutting toward one end until you are about two-thirds of the way along a piece of work, then reverse the cut to finish off the uncut section and blend in the two sections.

As with all fluted tools, the flute should point in the direction of the cut and the cut should take place on the lower wing of the tool **2**. The handle should be kept low and as close to the body. At first, the tool needs to come into contact with the rotating work without cutting. To do this, introduce the heel of the bevel to the rotating wood **3**.

You will hear a ticking noise **4**. This is the heel making contact with the corners of the wood. When you hear it, raise the handle until the cutting edge touches the wood **5**. When the cut begins, do not raise the handle any further **6** but move the tool along the rest, rotating the blade to alter the cut **7**. Move the tool along the rest in a controlled way and stop just off the end of the work **8**. A side view gives a clearer picture: the heel touching **9**; raising the handle and bringing the bevel into contact **10**; raising the handle just a little more bringing the cutting edge into play **11**; and the blade moving along the work **12**.

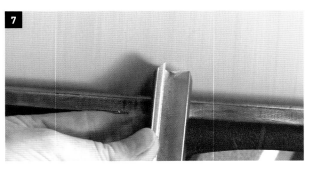

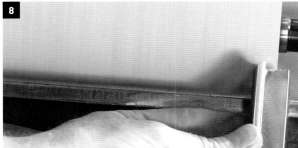

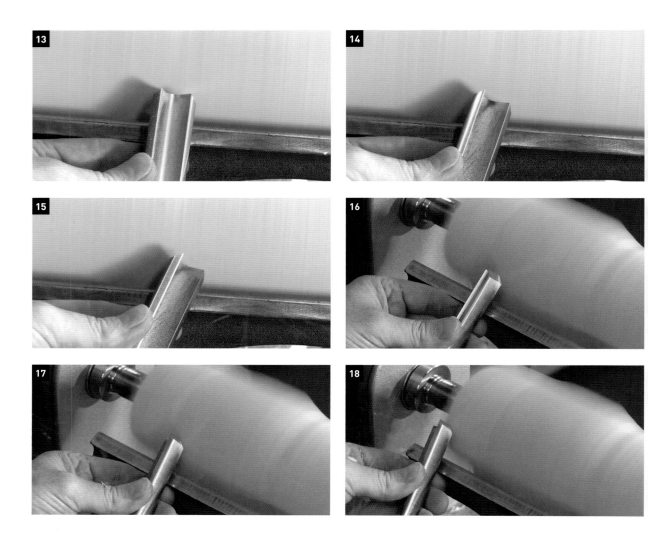

You can use the gouge square-on to the work **13**, or you can shift your body so you are at a slight angle to it **14**; this changes the cutting angles a little and produces a slightly better shearing cut **15**. When you have made multiple cuts and reached about two-thirds of the way along the work **16**, reverse the tool and the direction of the cut and start to smooth out the rest of the piece **17**, stopping often to see how you progress **18**. If you see any flats, just keep cutting **19** until the whole piece is a smooth cylinder, adjusting the direction of the cut as necessary to blend in the various cut parts **20**.

If you wish, you can refine the cut even more. This technique is best used as a finishing cut or when you are cutting timber that splinters and fractures easily. Incline the handle to about 45°; the flute should be pointing in the direction of the cut. Rotate the blade so that the flute is farther down—nearer the 8 o'clock or 4 o'clock position, depending on the direction of the cut **21**. The bevel is still rubbing during the cut, and this angle creates a shearing cut that peels the fibers off as the wood runs down the long edge presented to the work but is fully controllable and is handy to know when you need just a bit of surface refinement **22**.

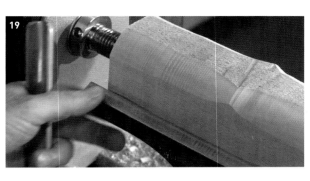

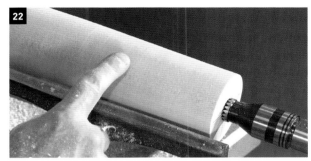

SWEEPING CURVES

You can cut sweeping curves with this tool using the cutting techniques already described **1**, but you must never cut uphill when spindle turning. Always stop at the lowest part of the curve **2** and if the shape is an elongated, cove-like form, reverse the tool and cut to meet the lowest section. Now you are cutting downhill and have the support of a longer fiber behind the one being cut **3**.

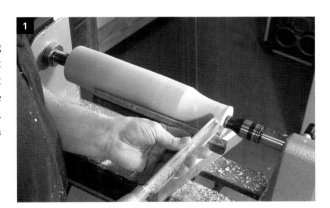

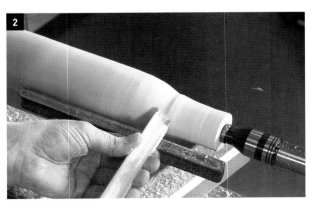

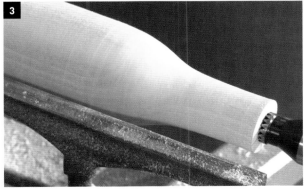

USING BEADING AND PARTING TOOLS

Parting tools and beading and parting tools may differ in shape and width of the cutting edge but are essentially similar, and the same cutting techniques can be used for both. These tools are often used to cut grooves, to part (cut off) the work from the waste section, and to cut beads, fillets, quirks, round tenons, and so on. They have their uses in both spindle and bowl work and most turners have a thin parting tool and a wider beading and parting tool to cope with all situations.

PARTING CUTS

The cleanest cut is made when the tool is used in bevel-rubbing mode. To do this, as with the spindle roughing gouge, the heel of the tool **1** should come into contact with the work first and the handle is low to start with **2**.

To start the cut, position the cutting edge horizontally to the work, support the blade on the rest, and use either the overhand or underhand grip. Apply enough downward pressure on the tool to keep the blade in contact with the rest while allowing you to move the tool as necessary. Ensure that the toolrest is set below center and the cutting edge of the tool is above center. The handle should be kept low and as close to the body as possible. Move the tool toward the work so the heel comes into contact with the rotating wood. You will hear a ticking noise. Keep the tool on the rest, press the heel lightly onto the wood, and then raise the handle until the cutting edge comes into contact with the wood.

Next, raise the handle and arc the tool into the wood, maintaining bevel contact all the time. Stop at the depth you require **3**. If you are making a very deep cut, you may experience binding on the blade. If this occurs, make a small clearance cut to the waste side of the cut to allow the blade to travel unimpeded during the primary cut **4**. If you need to part off the work when turning between centers, it is best to leave a small stub of wood. Switch off the lathe and use a saw to saw it off later. This is the safest method.

A side view clearly shows the arcing path of the cut. Present the tool heel first and raise the handle to get the bevel rubbing. When the bevel is rubbing, raise the handle a little more to make the cut. Arc the blade into the wood, moving the blade forward all the time **5**, until you reach the required depth **6**. You may end up losing the bevel rub at the final stage of the cut and end up with a scraping cut.

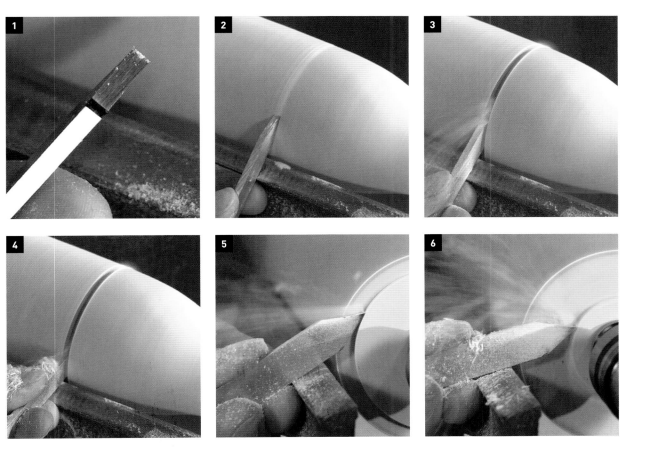

SCRAPING CUT OR PUSH CUT

Sometimes called a plunge cut, a scraping cut or push cut is similar to a parting cut; it is made with the handle low but without the bevel rubbing **1**. The angle at which the cutting edge is presented to the work means that at no time during the cut do we achieve the bevel-rubbing effect we have seen previously **2**. The scraping cut is cruder than the bevel-rubbing cut, but some turners find it easier to make certain cuts this way. The entry into the wood and the surface finish are often not as good with this type of cut, but it is a technique worth knowing, and it can be used on faceplate work too **3**.

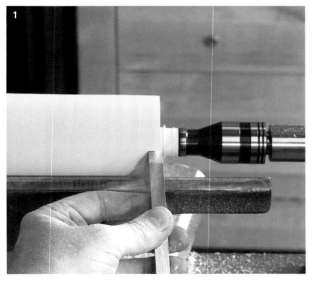

CUTTING TENONS OR SPIGOTS

Parting tools and beading and parting tools can also be used to cut tenons, also called spigots or fillets. This technique employs the same cutting action as the parting cut, but only to a limited depth. The tenon or fillet does not have to be parallel to the spindle; the blade can be moved to cut at any angle required. This is useful for creating dovetail tenons, for holding in chucks, and so on. Tenons or spigots are created by making a parting cut that stops short of going all the way through the depth of the work. Position the rest just below center, place the heel in contact with the work, and raise the handle to achieve a bevel-rubbing position. Raise the handle to get a cut **1** and arc the blade into the wood to the required depth **2**. Tilt the blade onto its corner and arc into the wood again to create the required angle on the dovetail cut **3**. Cut to the required depth and look at the profile to make sure it is what you require **4**.

MAKING V CUTS WITH THE BEADING AND PARTING TOOL

The wider section of the beading and parting tool gives you a bit more cutting edge to work with. To make a V cut, position the rest just below center height. Keep the handle low and the blade on the rest, pointing square on to the work, with the cutting edge vertical—that is, turned through 90° from the position used for the parting cut **1**.

Note that there is no heel to rub with this cut. Instead, when you are ready, advance the tool at about 45° to the work, make contact with the leading tip of the cutting edge, and raise the handle to arc into the cut. This incises a line by severing fibers and pushing the fibers to either side of the cutting edge as it goes in where the bevel is rubbing **2**.

If the V doesn't need to be very deep, you may not need to make additional cuts. But if you need to widen and deepen the cut, you can create the angled sides by positioning the blade so that you cut inline with the bevel at the correct angle. The cutting edge remains vertical and the leading tip of the cutting edge enters the wood **3**. Only the tip section should cut and you may need to angle the blade a little toward the chamfer you are cutting. About 5° is sufficient—any more and the cut will be made farther back on the cutting edge. This results in an aggressive cut that is difficult to control; and if you lose control, the edge then digs into the chamfer, creating a spiral spin out. So, enter the cutting tip in line with the bevel angle **4** and keep the cuts light and the cut on the tip section only **5**. Make multiple light cuts, working back from either side of the incised cut until you reach the width and depth required **6**. Only cut downhill and remember to arc the blade as you go deeper, but be careful. The deeper you go, the more likely you are to lose sight of the cutting tip **7**.

Practice these cuts over and over again until you are comfortable with the cutting positions and the movement during the cut **8**. The main thing to note is, apart from the tip section, keep to all parts of the cutting edge away from the timber to maintain control **9**.

CUTTING BEADS

You can also roll beads using the tip of the cutting edge. To practice this cut, make a parting cut on either side of what will be a bead, to create clearance for the tool, then mark the center of the bead form with a pencil.

Place the beading and parting tool on the rest so the corner of the cutting edge is about ¼in (6mm) from the edge of what will be the bead **1**. Keep the handle low, touch the wood with the heel of the bevel, raise the handle, and rotate the tool so the corner slices the wood **2**. Roll the tool so that the cutting edge arcs over the wood, with the very tip of the cutting edge severing the fibers of the wood **3**, until the cutting edge is in a position to finish the shape—this position can be almost vertical **4**. Repeat this process until you have shaped one side of the bead using successive light cuts, then shape and refine the other side of the bead, rolling the blade the other way **5**. Remember, do not make too big a cut. Many light cuts are better than one heavy cut and only the tip section or just a little behind it is used **6**.

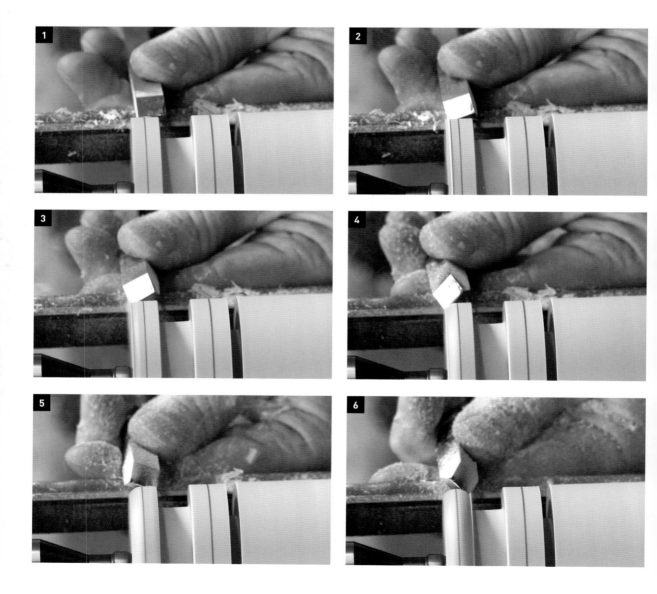

TECHNIQUE 6
USING SKEW CHISELS

The skew chisel is the equivalent of a woodworker's bench plane. It is an essential part of the spindle turner's armory for between-center work; it is not used on faceplate work. The tool is used to smooth the surface of the wood, incise V cuts, clean up end grain, roll beads, and make peeling cuts.

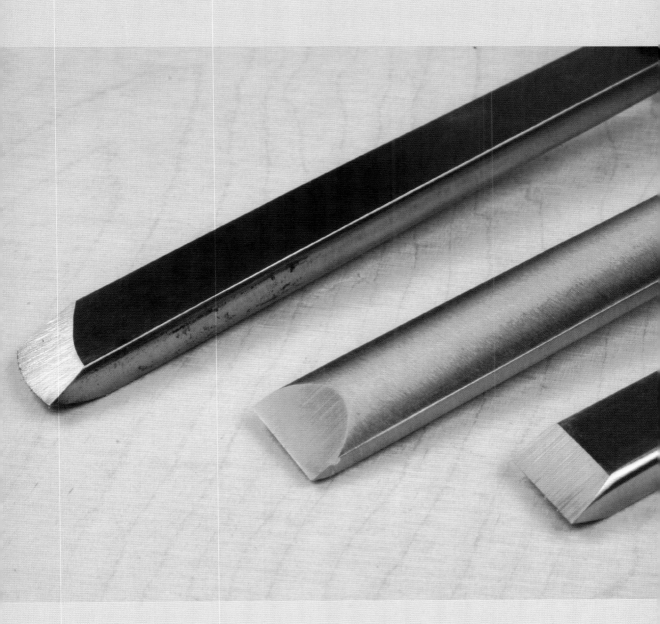

PLANING CUTS

The skew chisel has a long and a short point, sometimes called the toe and heel respectively. The heel on the cutting edge is not to be confused with the heel of the bevel.

Let's look at the planing cut with the long point uppermost. You can use the skew chisel with either the long or short point at the lowest part of the cutting edge, but it's usual to have the short point down. As with the spindle roughing gouge (see pages 61–5), do not cut into the end of the work; instead, start part of the way along it. I find that it is easier if the rest is placed above the center line. This means that when the blade is supported on the rest and presented to the work, the handle is closer to a horizontal position than some of the tools we have used so far. This enables you to support the handle closer in line with the arm and against the side of your body rather than down toward the hip **1**. The heel of the bevel is allowed to touch the wood, and the skew is angled so that when the handle is raised the cut occurs in the lower half of the blade (the section marked in black) **2**.

Position the skew edge at about 45° to the surface of the wood. If you do not cut using the lower half of the blade, the cutting edge is not properly supported by the section of the blade that is in contact with the rest, and the force of the cut may twist the blade a little—you may lose control of the cut and get a catch.

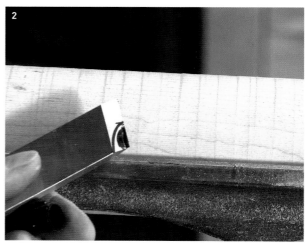

So, present the tool and raise the handle to make the bevel rub. Use the lower section of the cutting edge, just a little up from the heel, to make the cut. Move the blade across the work, maintaining the bevel-rub cut as you go. The cut occurs in the marked area, as evidenced by the dust line **3**.

By moving the handle position you can alter the presentation angle a little as you go, to create a more aggressive or more refined cut. The squarer the handle to the work, the coarser the cut; conversely, the closer the handle is to a horizontal position, the finer the cut will be **4**. Repeat the process, making as many light cuts as you need to ensure the surface is smooth **5**. Run off the end of the end of the work to make sure the surface is even and clean **6**. The planing cut can also be achieved with the toe down. Hold the handle at about 45° so the cutting edge is positioned at approximately 45° to the work; again, the cut occurs in the lower half of the cutting edge. To achieve a finer cut, move the handle closer to the horizontal. A coarser cut is achieved by moving the handle toward the vertical position **7**.

When one section of the spindle is clean, move the rest to a new section and repeat the process. If it is only the opposite end that you need to clean up, reverse the blade and cut that section, running the blade off the end of the work if possible, to ensure an even shape **8**.

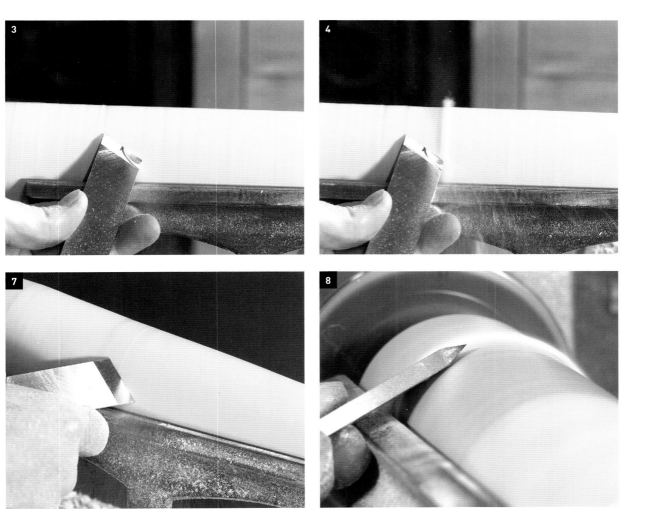

CLEANING UP END GRAIN

The skew chisel can also be used to clean up the end grain. For this task the tool is used long-point down, the rest is set on or just below the centerline, and the handle is held low toward the hip. Arc the edge into the wood, raising the handle as you go. To cut the wood, enter in line with the bevel with the cutting edge vertical **1** so that only the tip section is used; any other entry position will result in an uncontrollable cut. This is a bevel-rubbing cut, but only the lower shoulder of the bevel is touching the wood **2**.

You can see that only the very tip is cutting the wood; the rest of the cutting edge is held away from the wood. Start approximately 1/16in (1.5mm) away from the end of the work. Keep the handle low, enter the wood in line with the bevel, and keep the edge vertical; arc down toward the center of the work as the cut progresses **3**. Multiple light cuts, rather than one heavy cut, will give you more control and a cleaner cut. Again, it is vital that only the tip of the tool is used during the cut.

MAKING V CUTS

Making a V cut, typically done with the long point, is very similar to making a V cut with the beading and parting tool (see pages 66–71). Keep the handle low, the blade on the rest, square on to the work, and the cutting edge vertical (turned through 90° from the position used for the planing cut). Note that there is no heel to rub with this cut; instead, when you are ready, advance the tool at about 45° to the work, make contact with the leading tip of the cutting edge, and then raise the handle to arc into the cut **1**. This incises a line by severing fibers, pushing the fibers to either side of the cutting edge as it goes in.

As with the beading and parting tool, if the V doesn't need to be deep you may not need to make further cuts. But if you need to widen and deepen the cut, create the angled sides by angling the blade so you cut in line with the bevel at the correct angle. Keep the blade vertical, with the long point down, and cut into the wood. Only the tip section should cut; you may need to angle the blade in toward the chamfer by 5° or so **2**; any more and the cut will occur farther back on the cutting edge. This will result in an aggressive cut that is difficult to control, and the edge may roll into the chamfer, creating a spiral spin out. Keep the cuts light and the cut on the tip section only. Make multiple light cuts, working back from either side of the incised cut **3**, until you reach the width and depth required **4**. Only cut downhill. Practice these cuts until you are comfortable with the cutting positions and movement. Making deep V cuts is easier with a skew than with a beading parting tool.

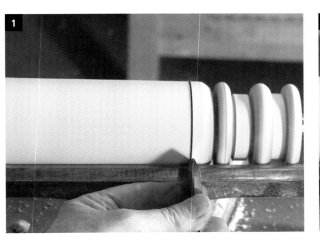

CUTTING BEADS

Rolling beads with a skew is similar to rolling beads with the beading and parting tools. The cut is usually made with the short point of the cutting edge down, but it can be made with the long point down **1**. Roll beads using the very tips of each end of the cutting edge.

To practice this cut, make a parting or V cut on either side of what will become a bead, to create clearance for the tool. Mark the center of the bead form with a pencil. Set the rest at about center height. Keep the handle low and place the skew on the rest with the corner of the cutting edge about ¼in (6mm) from the edge of what will be the bead. Touch the wood with the heel of the bevel, raise the handle to get a cut on the tip section, and rotate the tool so the corner slices the wood as it arcs over, until you reach the corner of the

V cut **2**. Make successive cuts, repeating this rolling motion and removing small amounts of wood each time, gradually forming one side of the bead. The cutting edge will end in an almost vertical position **3**.

When you have shaped one side, repeat the process for the other side with the skew edge pointing the other way **4**. Some people find cutting one direction easier than the other **5**, but your confidence will increase with practice and the results are well worth the time and effort **6**.

A side view of cutting the bead shows how the bevel rubs on the work before the lower point of the cutting edge comes in to make the cut, as the handle is raised just a little **7**. Then the blade is rolled **8** **9** until the bead is formed. The cutting edge is almost vertical at the bottom of the bead **10**.

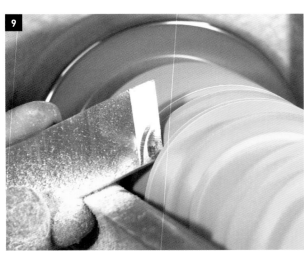

GENTLE CURVES

You can also use the skew to create sweeping curves. Remember to keep either the long or short point down—although more commonly done with the short point down—keeping the cut in the lower half of the cutting edge **1**. Always cut towards the lowest part of the curve **2**. Depending on the shape required, stop at the end of the curve or reverse the tool and work from the other side **3**.

PEELING CUT

There is one more cut that the skew is often used for—the peeling cut. This can be used to reduce square sections to round, and to create tenons **4**. Keep the handle low and square to the work, position the rest just below the centerline, and present the cutting edge horizontally or at a slight angle to the face being cut. Place the heel of the bevel against the work, raise the handle so that the bevel is rubbing, then raise it a little more to make the cut **5**. Arc the blade in the wood **6** just as you did for the end grain cut.

CURVED-EDGE SKEW

All the standard-grind skew chisel techniques on these pages can also be applied to the curved skew, but bear in mind that the curvature of the cutting edge changes the handle position during cutting. Planing cuts can be made with either the short or the long point down **1 2**. V Cuts are made with the with the long point down **3**. Beads can also be rolled using either the long or short point. The skew is ideal for creating large beads **4**.

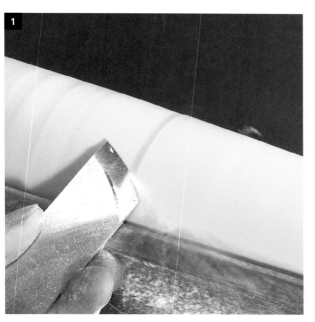

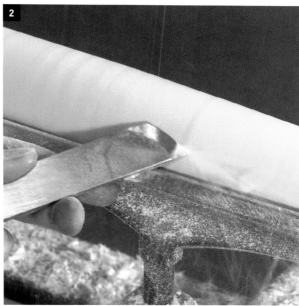

USING SPINDLE GOUGES

The spindle gouge is a very effective shaping and refining tool, capable of the most delicate of cuts for creating coves, beads, and curves. But, when necessary, and depending on the diameter of the blade, it can also be used for the bulk removal of waste timber.

GENERAL GUIDELINES

The spindle gouge is a bevel-rubbing tool. As shown in the sharpening section (see pages 40–53), it is commonly ground to a fingernail profile, which allows you to use various parts of the cutting edge to achieve the cut and shape required. It is worth noting that the very tip of the cutting edge is often not used. The cut is usually made just off to either side, depending on which way the flute is pointing. As with the spindle roughing gouge, the flute points in the direction of the cut and the cut occurs on the lower wing. By now, you may have started to notice similarities in the way that the various tools are used.

CUTTING A COVE

Cutting a cove with a spindle gouge is similar to making a V cut with a skew chisel. Mark the width of the cove, set the rest to just below the centerline of the spindle, and have the flute pointing in the direction of travel—so if you are cutting from the right side of the cove, the flute will point to the 9 o'clock position.

Enter the wood in line with the bevel **1**. The cut should be made about ¼in (6mm) from the tip on the lower wing **2**. Roll and rotate the blade as you progress through the cut to the deepest part of the cove—assuming you start cutting from the right side of the cove, the flute position **3** changes from the 9 o'clock position at the beginning of the cut to 10 o'clock part way down the side **4**, and nearer to the 11 o'clock position at the bottom of the cut **5**.

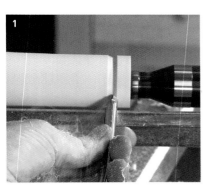
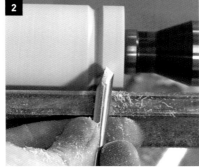

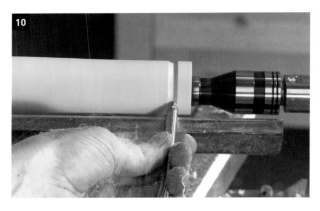

When this cut is complete, repeat the cutting sequence for the left side. This time, the flute starts at somewhere near the 3 o'clock position **6** and is rotated during the cut, moving through the 2 o'clock position as you near the lower section of the cove **7** in a controlled manner **8**, until it is nearer to the 1 o'clock position at the bottom **9**. Extend the depth and width of the cove with alternating left and right cuts until you reach the depth and width required **10**. You need to be very careful not to allow the leading cutting edge to come in to contact with the opposite side of the cove when you are at the bottom of the cut. Only cut downhill using a rotating scooping cut. A similar movement is made with the gouge that one would use if scooping ice-cream—starting on either outside edge of the scoop **11**.

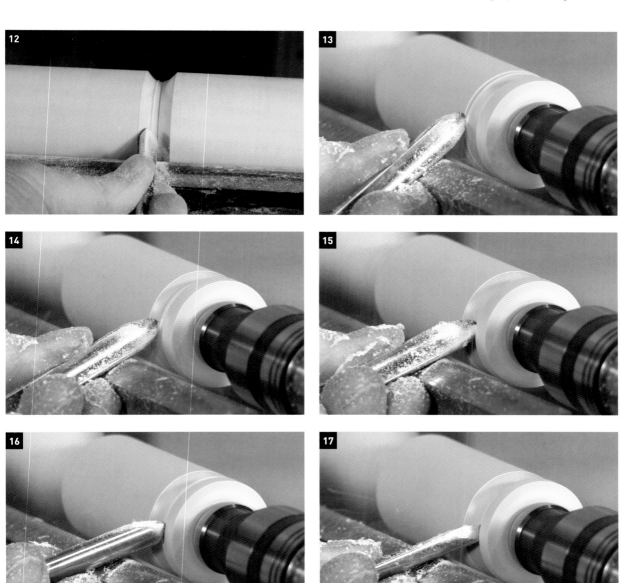

A useful little trick for cutting coves is to make a very thin parting cut to the depth required in the center of the cove with a parting tool, and then use this as a guide to the depth of cut required. This can save a lot of measuring and re-measuring **12**. A side view shows the cut starting on the left side of the cove. Note that the cut occurs about ⅛in (3mm) down from the tip of the tool. The flute position is at about 3 o'clock **13**. You can see the rotation of the blade through the 2 o'clock position **14**, which causes the cutting edge to follow a continuous curving path until you reach the bottom, and the flute is somewhere near the 1 o'clock position **15**. Once this side is cut, the other side is cut **16** until you are happy with the shape **17**.

CUTTING BEADS

Part down either side of the bead to be cut to give you clearance, or create a V cut with a skew chisel or parting tool, or with the spindle gouge. Set the rest just below centerline of the work. Place the spindle gouge on the rest, positioned so the cutting edge is about ¼in (6mm) from the edge of what will be the bead, and the flute is pointing straight up in the 12 o'clock position **1**. Keep the handle low, touch the wood with the heel of the bevel, and raise the handle to get the bevel rubbing. Rotate the tool either left or right as required, so the cutting edge—about ⅛–¼in (3–6mm) down from the tip—touches the wood, then roll the tool over so the edge slices the wood as it arcs over the corner of the work. The tool is not only rolled over, but the handle is also swung out. The amount of swing out is determined by

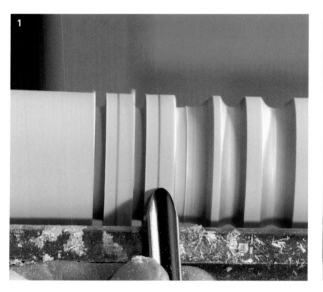

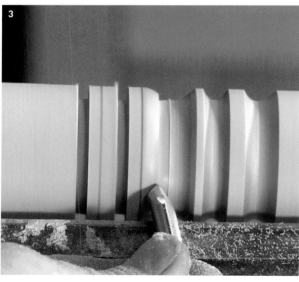

the bevel angle and also how deep you are going **2**. Repeat this shaping cut and adjust the handle position to maintain a controlled cut **3**. As you near the final depth of cut, the flute will lay almost horizontal, over to one side—almost in the 9 o'clock or 3 o'clock position, depending on which side of the bead you have cut **4**. When you've cut one side of the bead, repeat the sequence on the other side, once again working from the centerline of the bead **5**. You will need to rotate the blade **6**, and, depending on the width of the bead, you may need to slide the tool along the rest as you do so to form the bead shape properly **7**. Continue cutting on either side until you are happy with the shape of the bead **8**. The handle will once again swing over to allow a controlled bevel-rub-cut.

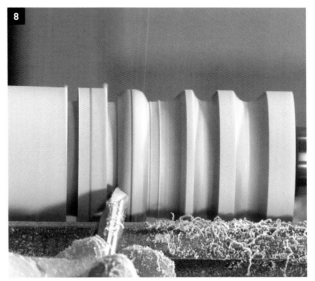

SWEEPING CURVES

To create sweeping curves, place and support the tool on the rest as already described for cutting coves and beads. Point the flute in the direction of the cut, and manipulate the cutting edge by adjusting the handle and flute position as you guide the tool along the work **1**. Remember to cut downhill **2**, never uphill, and always make the cut on the lower wing of the cutting edge **3**.

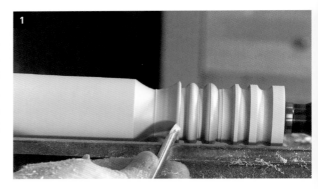

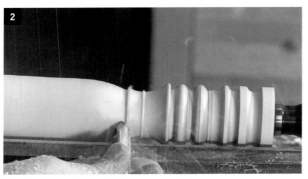

CUTTING END GRAIN

To create a straight cut across the face of the end of the spindle, position the rest just below center height. Have the flute pointing in the direction of travel and keep the handle low so that the cut takes place on the lower wing of the tool, about ⅛in (3mm) from the tip **4**. Pull the blade along the rest a little past the edge of the work. Move the blade forward a fraction then push forward along the rest to enter the wood in line with the bevel **5**, then arc the blade across the face until you cut down onto the very center **6**. There is no need to alter the flute position as you arc across the face. You can also cut curves in this way, but you will need to alter the handle height and flute position depending on the depth of the cut. These movements are very similar to those used in cutting coves and curves.

TECHNIQUE 8
USING SCRAPERS

Scrapers are refining tools, used after the main shaping has been done. They are primarily used for bowl work, but can also be useful for some spindle work, such as goblets and boxes. Scrapers are best used on close-grained hardwoods.

GENERAL GUIDELINES

Scrapers are not used with the bevel rubbing. For maximum control, they are placed flat on the rest and used with a trailing blade angle. If the tool is held horizontally, or even pointed upward, the cut is aggressive and is likely to be too big and difficult to control, which may result in a catch that causes the edge to dig in and be pulled down into the wood.

The scraper used should match the profile of the work being refined. If the external surface of the bowl has both internal and external curves (concave and convex) as with an ogee shape, for example, then you will need to use a curved scraper as well as a square end/angled scraper. It is also advisable to use the widest possible blade to ensure the smoothness of the shape. Using a small blade on large curves is likely to create ridges, not remove them.

EXTERNAL CURVES

An angled or square-profile scraper is used for external work such as a gently curved bowl. However, if you have two opposite curves running together—an ogee, for example—you will need to use a curved scraper too. Set the rest on or just below center. Place the blade flat on the rest. Raise the handle so the blade tilts downward a little, so that the cut will occur on or just below the center line of the work **1**.

Push the blade gently into the wood until the tool starts to cut, and move the tool into or across the work as necessary to refine the shape. Only the gentlest of touches is required **2**. The cutting action of a scraper is not as refined as that of a gouge, and a scraper is best used on close-grained dense timbers. To minimize tearout, always cut in such a way that there is a longer fiber behind the one being cut. In the case of external bowl work, cut from the smallest to the largest section—downhill—so the blade is traversed around the piece to refine the external curve **3**.

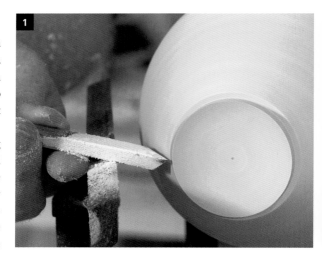

INTERNAL CURVES

For internal bowl work, set the rest on or just above the centerline. The cut is made on or just above center. Remember, the blade must trail down in order to give you maximum control. To ensure a well-supported cut, move the scraper from the largest outer section near the rim down toward the inner, lower section. This too can be viewed as a downhill movement **1**.

END-GRAIN CURVES

For end-grain spindle work such as goblets and boxes, the scraper is usually only used to refine the hollow internal shapes. Present the blade in the same way as you would for bowl work, but make the cut from the lower inner section of the work **2** out toward the upper rim section **3**.

SHEAR SCRAPING

Shear scraping occurs when the angle of the cutting edge is inclined in relation to the work to create a peeling-type cut. Imagine a knife slicing through bread—you're trying to create that slicing action. This is a more refined cut; the bevel does not rub and the blade trails, as with the standard scraping cut. However, as with a skew chisel, keep the cut in the lower half of the cutting edge for optimal control **1**.

The scraper blade is tilted so the flat face points in the direction of the cut, and is presented at approximately a 45° angle **2**. The blade trails backward slightly **3** and is pulled around the work **4**. A finer cut can be achieved when the cutting edge is closer to a vertical position. The closer that the cutting edge gets to the horizontal, the coarser the cut will be—just like a normal scraping cut.

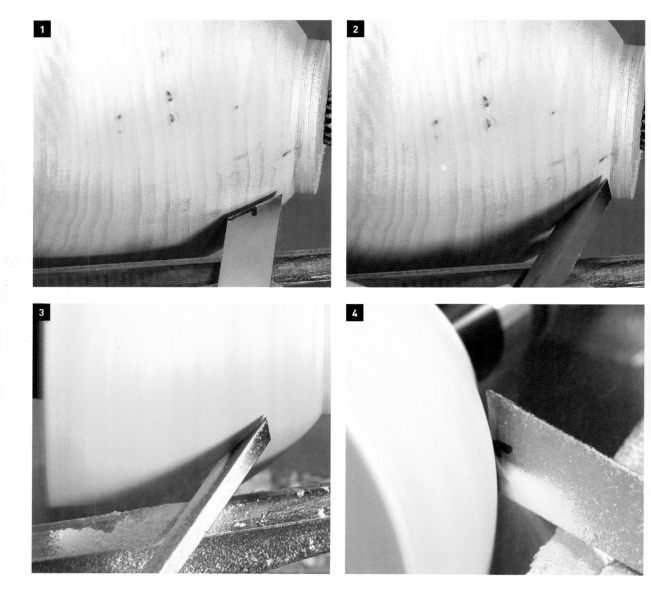

USING BOWL GOUGES

As the name implies, bowl gouges are usually used for bowls and other faceplate work, but they can be used for some spindle work too. As the bowl turner's primary shaping tools, they are used to remove excess wood, but can also be employed with great finesse to refine the work after initial shaping.

EXTERNAL SHAPING

Like the other bevel-rubbing tools, the bowl gouge enters the wood in line with the bevel. The rest is below center, and the cut occurs on or just above the centerline of the work.

As with a spindle gouge, point the flute in the direction of the cut at approximately the 10 o'clock position, so the cut is made on the lower wing of the cutting edge. For the smoothest results, cut with the grain **1**, from the smallest to the largest section—which is downhill. Keep the handle low and inclined at an angle of about 45° **2**.

Start by nibbling off the corners with what are effectively chamfer cuts. Make straight cuts across the wood, removing waste material quickly as you make multiple passes **3**. Altering the flute to nearer the 11 o'clock position will give you a more aggressive cut, but you risk making the cut on the uppermost wing of the cutting edge; this will alter the

cutting forces and may twist the blade into the cut, resulting in a catch. Pointing the flute closer toward the horizontal 9 o'clock position will give you more of a scraping cut.

When you're ready to make a curved cut, enter the wood as before, but instead of pushing the blade in a straight line, swing the handle toward your body to create the curve radius you require **4**. This may take a little practice, but just make sure you maintain the bevel rub **5**; this enables you to control the tool by rotating the blade, raising or lowering the handle, and pushing the blade in the correct direction, depending on the shape being cut **6**.

You can create deeper, quicker shaping cuts by going farther into the wood with the cutting edge. This is great for shaping, but for a more refined result, cuts of about ⅛in (3mm) deep will clean up the surface more effectively **7**.

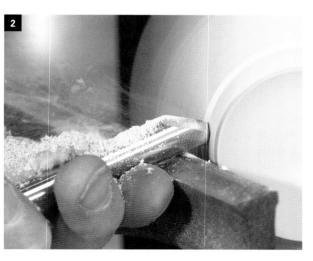

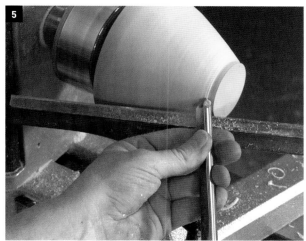

INTERNAL SHAPING

For internal bowl work, set the rest just below center, cutting just above the centerline of the work and make the cut from the surface down into the center section of the work. The bevel rubs for this cut. Keep the gouge stable on the rest. Point the flute in the direction of the cut, somewhere near the 2 o'clock position, and enter in line with the bevel **1**. When the cut has started, the bevel rub will allow you to pull the handle toward you as you cut to create the required curve **2**. Work on the center area first; when this cut is complete, make successive cuts back toward the outer rim **3**. Always work from the top, face down toward the center section, being careful not to cut too deep at the bottom **4**.

You can alter the flute position to create a heavier or lighter cut, but always have the flute pointing in the direction of the cut and make the cut on the lower wing of the cutting edge. These rules should be followed whether you are cutting across the work in a flat plane, creating curved cuts, or cutting S-shaped curves.

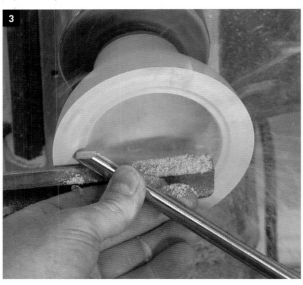

PULL CUT

A pull cut can be used to quickly shape or subtly refine the work. It can be made with or without the bevel rubbing, although it is more often used without. This makes it useful when the tailstock is in position to provide support, or when cutting up against a spigot, when it is difficult to get the handle position in the correct place for a bevel-rubbing cut. It can also be used without the tailstock in place, but if the cut is used without the bevel rubbing, the resulting surface will not be as clean as with a bevel-rubbing cut.

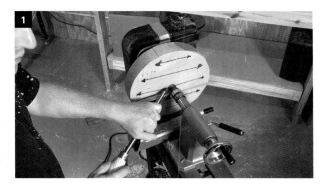

To make a pull cut, hold the tool handle close to the hip and position it at approximately 45°. Present the gouge to the work so that the flute is pointing at approximately the 10 o'clock position **1**. The cut is made on the lower edge; gently touch the heel of the bevel and roll the blade until you have a cut then pull it along the work **2**.

Due to the angle of approach, the flute is still pointing in the direction of the cut. You can create a more aggressive cut by raising the handle toward the horizontal, but take care, as this is an aggressive cut that can be tricky to control. A finer cut can be made by lowering the handle so the approach angle is nearer the 60°–45° position.

Making this cut without the bevel rubbing gives it a scraping-cut effect. Rotate the blade so the flute points closer toward the work. Pointing the flute toward the 11 o'clock position will mean that the bevel will be almost rubbing, but not quite. A combination of raising and lowering the handle and rotating the blade will alter the cut as required **3**. Experiment with this cut and you are likely to find it useful in some situations.

SHEAR SCRAPE

The scraping cut described above can be adjusted to create a fine, peeling shave that is used to refine the surface prior to sanding. Keep the handle low toward the hip. Present the cutting edge at an approximately 45° angle to the work with the flute pointing almost into the work, but not quite **4**. The cut takes place on the lower edge, and the tool is drawn across the face of the work, working with the grain. Raising or lowering the handle will create a finer or coarser cut.

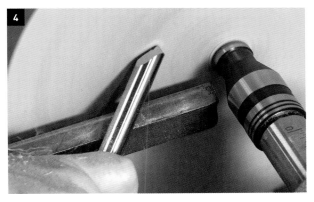

PROJECT 1

CLASSICAL FORM BOWL

We use bowls all the time in daily life, and aside from their very obvious practical functions they can also be things of beauty. In this project we are going to make a bowl based on a classical form called an ogee.

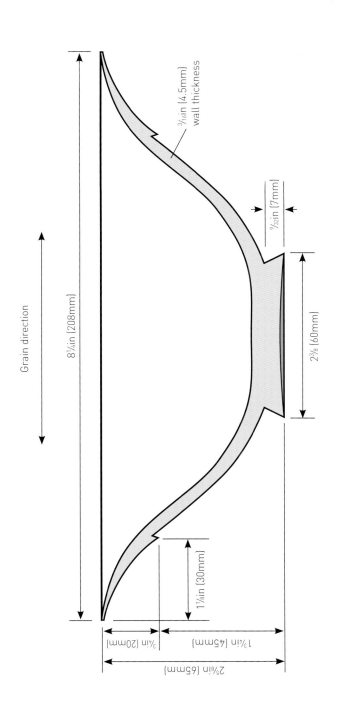

Grain direction

8¼in (208mm)

³⁄₁₆in (4.5mm)
wall thickness

⁹⁄₃₂in (7mm)

2³⁄₈ (60mm)

1⅛in (30mm)

¾in (20mm)

1¾in (45mm)

2⅝in (65mm)

DIMENSIONAL DIAGRAM OF BOWL

MAKING THE BOWL

An ogee is effectively a S-curve profile, which is a versatile shape to experiment with as it can be squashed, made taller, or stretched as you wish. The timber I have used is carob, but you can pick a different timber if you like—however, it is easier and more common to use a hardwood for this type of work. The blank is about 9in (230mm) across and just under 3in (75mm) thick **1**. While choosing your blank, check it over for splits, flaws or bark inclusion. When you're satisfied that there are none that will cause a problem, you can start considering your chucking and orientation options. Because of the bark, this face is going to be the bottom of the bowl and will be turned and shaped first. The other side is the top section of the bowl **2**. It is going to be mounted on a screwchuck attachment that fits in a chuck, but you could also use an independent screwchuck or a faceplate for this if you choose. The hole used for the screwchuck, or the holes left by screws in a faceplate, will eventually be turned away when you turn the inside of the bowl. The other area will be the underside of the bowl. Find and mark the center of the blank—or as close to the center as possible. Drill a hole the correct size for the screw of the screwchuck **3**. Make the hole deep enough to accept the screw, but no deeper.

Wind the wood onto the screw fully into the hole and make sure that the face of the bowl sits squarely against the edges of the jaws, and that it does not rotate or wobble **4**. In this instance the hold is secure, but we are going to use the tailstock for support while we shape the underside of the bowl. (You do not have to use the tailstock if you find it easier not to and you have a secure enough hold from your screwchuck fixing.) Set the toolrest so that it is parallel to the exposed flat face of the blank and adjust the rest so that it is about ¼in (6mm) below center and just far enough away that it will not foul the blank when it is turned by hand. If you have any areas of bark or bark inclusion, check that the pieces are secure and not likely to fly off when you start the lathe. In this case the bark was loose, so I removed it **5**. Before starting the lathe, read the safety guidelines and make sure you are following them. When you've done so, select a speed appropriate for your blank size and condition and switch on the lathe **6**. I chose a speed of 800 rpm, but adjust this up or down a little if you encounter vibration. The blank was not flat on this bottom face, and the tailstock was in position for support, so I used a pull cut to flatten off the face. Remember to keep the handle low and the flute

pointing in the direction of the cut. The blade should be positioned at a presentation angle of approximately 45°. The bevel does not need to rub for this cut. Next, cut a spigot or tenon on the bottom of the body shape to suit the jaws you are using, so the bowl can be held in a chuck to turn the inside later. Use a pencil to mark the areas you need to cut. The diagram on page 99 shows the shape of the underside of the bowl and the cuts that we will make in order to shape the bowl. The cuts are made in such a way that there are supporting fibers behind the fiber being cut—cutting downhill, in other words. The spigot or tenon needs to be large enough to support the work while we cut the inside. It will also become the base of the bowl. Most utilitarian items—bowls and platters that are used to hold food and other items—have a base size of between a third and a half of the overall diameter to make the item stable. Platters are low and shallow, so you cannot see the base unless you turn over the work. This allows you to select a base diameter that suits the work. However, on bowls such as this you can see the base easily, so bases tend to be nearer to a third of the overall diameter. As a rough guide, this proportion will serve you well until you develop your skills further.

Make sure the jaw set you use is able to cater for the tenon or spigot size required. Then, take a ⅛in (3mm) parting tool and make a plunge cut on the outer mark of the spigot to a depth of about ⅜in (10mm) **7**. Present the tool with the handle held low and the blade supported on the rest. Arc into the work to the depth required; the bevel does not rub. You can raise the handle to create more of a scraping cut or lower the handle to create a better shear cut. When you reach the required depth, stop the lathe and move the rest. You have now defined the spigot section and you have a visual marker for where to cut to when shaping the outside. With the work stationary set the rest at a 45° angle across the corner of the blank, just below the centerline and just far enough away so the blank does not foul the rest when rotated by hand. Take your bowl gouge and place it on the rest so the flute is pointing to about 10 o'clock and in the direction of the cut. Keep the handle low and enter the wood in line with the bevel **8**. Make multiple ⅛–¼in (3–6mm) push cuts straight across this corner to remove the bulk of the waste quickly and easily. You can use this waste wood to practice adjusting the angle of the handle and/or the flute position to achieve the smoothest cut possible.

Always have in mind the shape you wish to cut **9**. If you cut off too much wood, you cannot replace it and the shape of the bowl would have to be modified accordingly. Stop the lathe after a few cuts and move the rest closer to the work so the overhang of the tool is not too great. With the bulk of the waste material removed, stop the lathe and reposition the rest so you can access the spigot section and reach as far around the work as possible. Take a bowl gouge and, starting close to the spigot, make a push cut to remove the waste close to the spigot. Then use a series of pull cuts followed by push cuts to shape the blank further **10**.

Start creating the S-curve by moving the handle or shifting your body slightly to direct the cut **11**. Practice these cuts now while there is waste wood available. It doesn't matter if you make a mistake as long as you don't go too deep into the section we need for the final shape. About one-third of the way down from the top rim section, create a step fillet **12**. This provides a visual and tactile break in the flow of the S-curve. It doesn't have to be very deep, and surprisingly the S-curve is still fully visible, with no jarring transition. Use a push cut with a parting tool to create the correct form for your jaws on the tenon **13**. Then use a pull cut with a

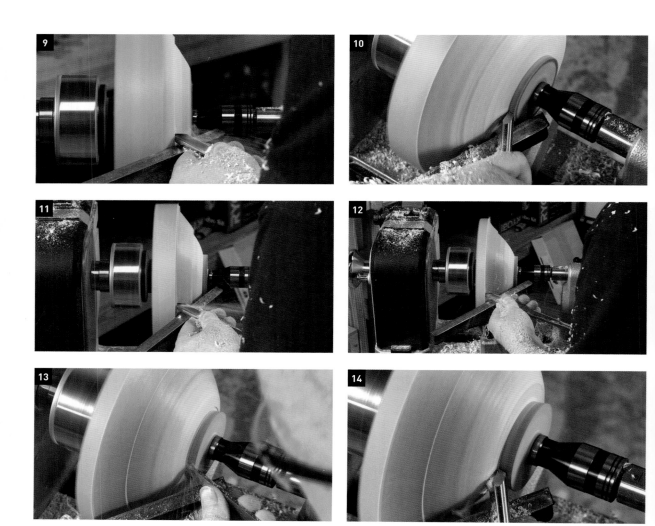

bowl gouge to blend in the base area with the main body curve **14**. Use a push cut to refine the shape. Make very small, gentle cuts **15**. Adjust the outward part of the S-curve to suit the shape you require. Note that the edge of this section of the curve comes out of the side of the blank and not out of the top **16**. This method allows you to use as much of the height of the blank as you need—just because you bought a blank three inches high doesn't mean you have to use all of it if it compromises the shape you want. Going through the side of the blank also gives you the maximum width to play with. Some turners make a final cleaning skim cut using a standard ground gouge, but this is not compulsory—find out what suits you **17**. When you are happy with the shape, examine it to see how clean it is. If you cannot see any major damage, lumps and bumps, or grain tearout, you can go straight to using abrasive. Otherwise, use an appropriate scraper to clean up the curve or surface. Remember to tilt the blade downward **18**. If you think you can get a better surface finish by using a shear scraping cut then do so, but trail the blade and only cut using the lower part of the cutting edge **19**. If necessary, use a round-nose or French-curve scraper for the outward curve (see page 90) **20**.

Use a shear scrape cut if you think it will help refine the surface further **21**. When the shape is clean, it is time to use an abrasive. Keep the abrasive moving at all times and sand in the lower section of the work, between the 4 o'clock and 8 o'clock positions if possible. Remember to use extractors and masks as necessary to minimize your exposure to dust. Work through the grits to create a smooth, clean surface **22**. The choice of whether to use hand- or power-sanding techniques is yours. Take care not to sand off any fine detail. If you are power sanding, set the drill to run in contra-rotation to the lathe for the most effective abrading method **23**. When you are happy with the outside, remove the bowl from the screwchuck and remove the screw. Fit

the bowl into the chuck and grip it securely on the tenon cut **24**. Bring up the rest and rotate the work by hand to make sure the blank doesn't catch the rest. Now remove the internal section of the bowl using the cuts shown in the techniques section of this book. Keep the handle low and the flute pointing in the direction of the cut at the 2 o'clock position. Introduce the tool in line with the bevel and make the cut on the lower wing, working from the top face and arcing the movement by bringing the handle toward the body to create the curve **25**. A slower or quicker movement of the handle will create a longer or tighter curve respectively. Make consecutive arcing cuts, cutting deeper and working back toward the outer bowl rim area. Don't go beyond half

the full depth at this stage **26**. When you are nearing the outer rim area you can use a pull cut to refine the top, if it is not flat. This will help you see the edge more clearly and give you a more stable entry into the wood with the gouge **27**. Work back to the rim, remembering to leave some wall thickness in the bowl. Aim for ¼in (6mm) or slightly less, depending on how comfortable you are with the cuts you are making at this stage **28**. The cuts become easier with practice and as your tool control improves. Stop the lathe and check the wall thickness regularly, either by hand or using a measuring device. The next step is to refine the rim and the first part of the inner curve of the bowl **29**. Use a bowl gouge to remove any major ridges or curve deviations

and then a scraper, if required, to refine it further. Remember to cut with the grain, which means you push from the rim down into the inner body curve. You can use an angled scraper for the first part of the outward curved section **30**, but when the curve changes direction lower down you will need a curved or round-nose scraper. When you have refined the rim section and the first part of the inner body curve, use a gouge to remove the lower, uncut waste wood and create the lower curved part of the bowl **31**. At the very bottom the periphery speed is quite low. Lower the handle and arc down onto the center of the bowl—the technique is similar to the arcing cut of the parting tool, or cutting a tenon **32**. This is a more refined cut than just following

the push cut at the same height all the way through. Again, find what is comfortable for you. Next, if necessary, use a scraper to refine the curve and blend in the two sections **33**. Then remove the tailstock completely out of the way so as not to get in the way of you or the sanding process and use abrasives either with a hand- or power-sanding method to clean up the surface prior to applying a finish. Make sure you are using extraction and appropriate masks. You can see the dust coming off the work. Remember to work through the grits and sand in the lower section of the bowl between the 4 and 8 o'clock positions if you view the bowl as a clock face **34**. Don't be afraid to go back and refine or alter something if you need to. In this case, there was a flat spot near the rim

that was missed. Just make your adjustments and sand again until you are satisfied with the result **35**. Apply a finish that is appropriate for the intended use of the item and that will create the luster you want. I used an oil, which was applied using paper kitchen towels while the lathe was stationary. I then started the lathe and rubbed the paper towel over the surface to polish the bowl and remove any excess oil **36**. Remove the bowl from the lathe. There are jaw marks left on the tenon from the chuck. The tenon is going to be the base of the bowl, so it needs to be cleaned up. A good technique is to use a friction-drive between-center method. Take scrap piece of wood, hold it in the chuck, and cut a domed surface on it **37**. Then take some kitchen paper (four layers should

be enough), fold the layers together, and place them over the dome **38**. Place the inside of the bowl onto this paper on the domed surface you have just cut and bring up the tailstock to support it. You already have the center point marked from using the tailstock in the earlier stages **39**. Tighten everything up using enough pressure to allow the piece to spin without slipping when it is cut. This method can be used to hold all manner of work—all you have to do is adjust the size, shape, and length of the waste-wood drive. Use a gouge or parting tool to remove the damaging marks. This is going to be the foot so you can create whatever design of foot you like, but this one will retain a slight dovetail profile. Stop the lathe and check to see how you are getting on and adjust as necessary. Use a parting tool to remove the sharp corner of the new foot area. When happy, remove the rest and sand and blend the new section into the previously cut area and also slightly undercut the base, stopping just short of the revolving center **40**. Sand the whole of the outside of the work and apply your chosen finish **41**. When you've applied the finish, remove the piece from the lathe, cut off the small stub left where the tailstock holding the bowl in position and sand off any marks left and apply a finish on the sanded surface. Your bowl is now finished. You can see that the base is just under a third of the size but suits this bowl well. There is a lovely curve, and the step fillet does not overpower the visual line of the external curve **42**.

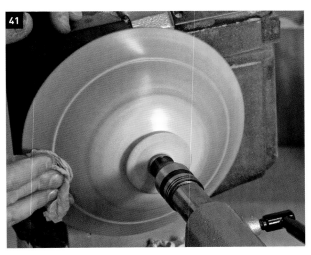

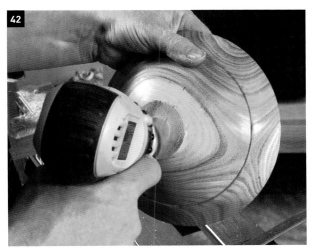

PROJECT 2
ROSEWOOD CANDLESTICK

Candlesticks make a great centerpiece for a table, and are an ideal way to practice the cuts and techniques shown earlier in the book. The example in this project is made from rosewood, but you can use any close-grained hardwood.

DIMENSIONAL DIAGRAM
OF CANDLESTICK

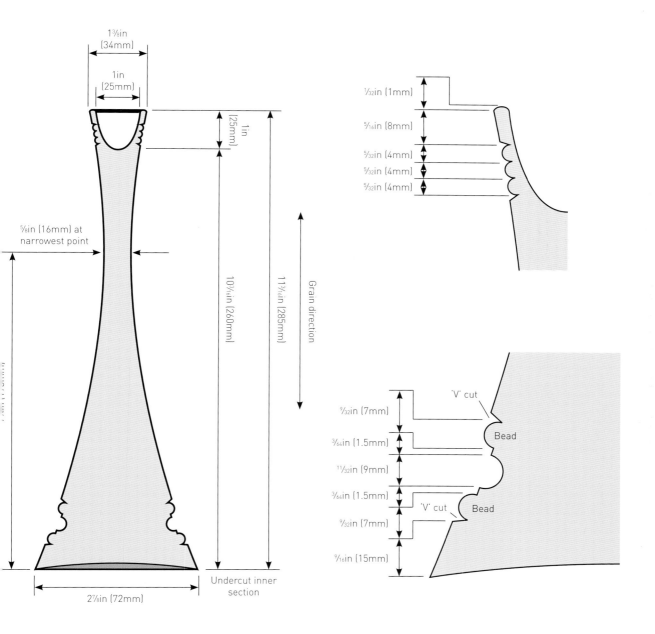

1³⁄₈in (34mm)

1in (25mm)

1in (25mm)

⁵⁄₈in (16mm) at narrowest point

10¹⁄₄in (260mm)

11³⁄₁₆in (285mm)

Grain direction

2⁷⁄₈in (72mm)

Undercut inner section

¹⁄₃₂in (1mm)

⁵⁄₁₆in (8mm)

⁵⁄₃₂in (4mm)

⁵⁄₃₂in (4mm)

⁵⁄₃₂in (4mm)

⁹⁄₃₂in (7mm)

³⁄₆₄in (1.5mm)

¹¹⁄₃₂in (9mm)

³⁄₆₄in (1.5mm)

⁹⁄₃₂in (7mm)

⁹⁄₁₆in (15mm)

'V' cut

Bead

'V' cut

Bead

MAKING THE CANDLESTICK

You will need a piece of timber 3 x 3 x 12in (75 x 75 x 300mm) long. I have used rosewood. The grain runs along its length and will be fixed between centers—a drive spur in the headstock and a revolving center in the tailstock **1**. Mark the centers on each end of the wood. A center finder is very useful for this task **2**. Fix the wood between centers on the lathe and adjust the rest so that it is just below the centerline and off to one end, ready for using a spindle roughing gouge **3**. When the rest is in place, spin the wood by hand to make sure it is clear of the rest, then switch on the lathe **4**. Use the spindle roughing gouge to remove the square edges. Remember: have the handle low until you hear the "tick" of the heel of the bevel touching the work, then raise the handle until you get a very slight cut on the cutting edge and then adjust the handle position to a coarse shaping cut or refined peeling cut as required **5**.

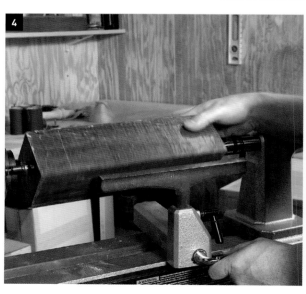

Remember: don't cut into the end grain, keep the flute pointing in the direction of the cut, and make the cut on the lower wing. Make multiple light cuts, starting from farther back along the wood each time, keeping the tool in contact with the rest at all times. You will reach a stage in which the wood on one side is tapered and almost round at the far end. At this point switch off the lathe, move the rest to the opposite end, and check that it doesn't foul the work. You are ready to cut this end **6**. Once again, the gouge should point in the direction the of cut. Make successive cuts to work your way back toward the other end—adjusting the rest as necessary to allow best access to the work—blending the two ends to create a cylinder of wood **7**. When you are happy with this cylinder, use the beading and parting tool to cut a tenon or spigot that will fit your chuck jaws on the tailstock end of the wood **8**.

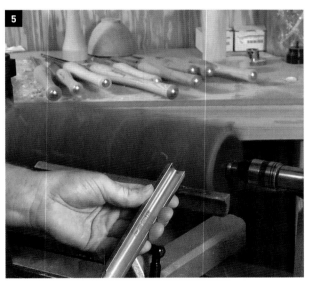

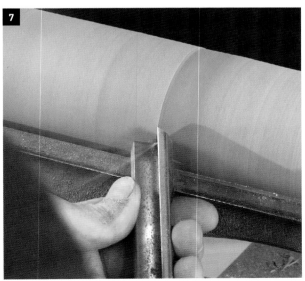

Remove the piece from the lathe and secure it in the chuck, making sure you tighten up the jaws properly and that the piece runs centrally. To help with this, bring up the tailstock—this will centralize the piece—and tighten up the chuck fully **9**. Use the spindle roughing gouge to roughly shape the candlestick **10**. The shape is like a long, sweeping cove. Part way through the rough shaping process, measure and mark a position one-third of the way down the cove—this will be the narrowest part of the curve and the transition point as the curve then sweeps the other way toward the base. Remember not to cut uphill, only downhill with the grain—so you need to cut from both sides, working down to the lowest part. Don't make the cylinder too thin at this stage—about 1¾in (43mm)

diameter at the curve transition point is fine. Use either a beading and parting tool or a spindle gouge to partly create the top curve of the candlestick. The shape is more or less half a bead so can be created with either tool. Remember, make light cuts and roll the blade as you cut to make sure you are cutting on the lower tip of the beading and parting tool, or the lower wing of the gouge **11**. Now for an end-grain hollowing cut, which we haven't shown yet but is very handy to know. Remove the tailstock ready to make the hollowing cuts to accept a candlestick metal cup. Take a spindle gouge, place it on the rest and adjust the height until the gouge is horizontal and aligned to the center of the work. The flute should point to approximately the 10 o'clock position, and the cut should

be made on the lower wing. Push the blade forward to create a hole of the correct depth. Pull the tool out and swing it out at the front section to cut the required opening size. Make small cuts until you reach the drilled depth **12**. Sand the hollow, using a French-curve scraper to refine the shape **13**. Stuff kitchen paper in the cut hole and bring up the tailstock. This will prevent the revolving center from marking the wood, but allow it to support and centralize the project. Use a spindle roughing gouge to refine the shape further. The critical part now is to get the correct curve and diameters at the top and bottom of the candlestick **14**. Measure and mark the position of the top three beads. Use a skew chisel to create small V cuts on each of the pencil marks **15**, then swap

to either a parting tool or a spindle gouge to roll the beads. These are small beads so only light cuts are needed. Take your time **16**. Clean up each end of the beads to create a chamfer. For the bottom area, measure and mark the positions of the coves and beads. Use a skew chisel to make V cuts, as for the top section **17**. Rough-shape the cove using a spindle gouge. Then, using a parting or beading and parting tool, cut the two outer beads. Only cut on the lower tip of the edge **18**. When the beads are cut, use a spindle gouge to deepen and refine the cove. Take care not to catch the lower wing on the opposite side of the cove **19**. Take a parting tool and cut down the side of the beads to create the fillets. Reshape the inner sides of the beads with a spindle gouge **20**.

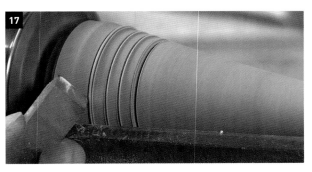

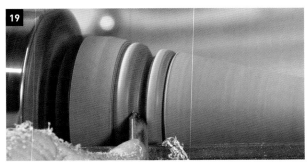

Take a look at the beads and coves at each end. Do not be afraid to go back and refine or alter the shapes as necessary. Here, the bead forms at the top seemed a bit too shallow, so I used a skew to deepen the sides a little, making the beads seem fuller and more defined **21**. Then refine the curve between the detailed areas to the final depth and shape required **22**. In readiness for removing the piece later on, take a parting tool and making a parting cut to about 1¾in (43mm) deep at the bottom section. Note there is a section

of timber directly in front of the chuck. You should not go too close to the jaws with a tool or you can catch the steel. Use the tool to just create a chamfer on the bottom outer edge **23**. You are now ready to sand the piece. Work through the grits, starting with the coarsest—120–150-grit is a good place to start—down to about 400-grit. Don't skip any grit grades and keep the abrasive moving at all times. Pay special attention to the detailed areas, and take care not to blur and soften the crisp detail you have already created **24**.

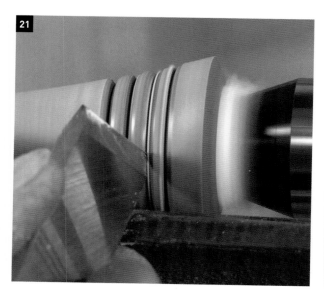

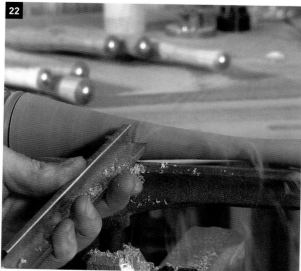

When the piece is smooth and free of any visible scratches left by the coarse abrasive, you can apply a finish. I used an oil and carefully applied it with kitchen towels while the work was stationary. But you can use other finishes to suit your personal likes and dislikes in terms of the luster achieved. Once the surface is completely coated, switch on the lathe to burnish the surface. Be careful as you draw near to the chuck. If you make contact with it, the cloth or paper is shredded very fast, so imagine what it could do to your skin. Go carefully **25**. After burnishing, switch off the lathe, and when the work is stationary move the rest to the chuck end. With a parting tool cut almost, but not quite, through the stub of wood left at the headstock end, stop the lathe, and then saw through the last bit **26**. When the candlestick is free, use a chisel or knife to clean up the stub, and a drill fitted with a sanding arbor to clean up the base **27**. Finally, oil the bottom and top hollow and your candlestick is finished **28**.

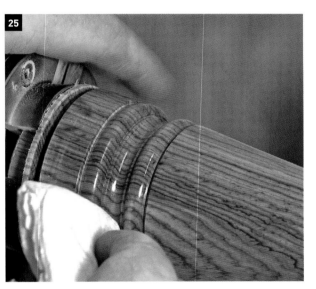

CYLINDRICAL BOX

Boxes are good fun to make. They make excellent presents and are perfect for storing rings, necklaces, and other small treasures. I chose to make this one from maple, but any close-grained hardwood would be suitable. A general rule of thumb for creating well-proportioned boxes is to have two-thirds of the height for the base and one-third for the lid; three-fifths and two-fifths is a good alternative.

DIMENSIONAL DIAGRAM OF BOX

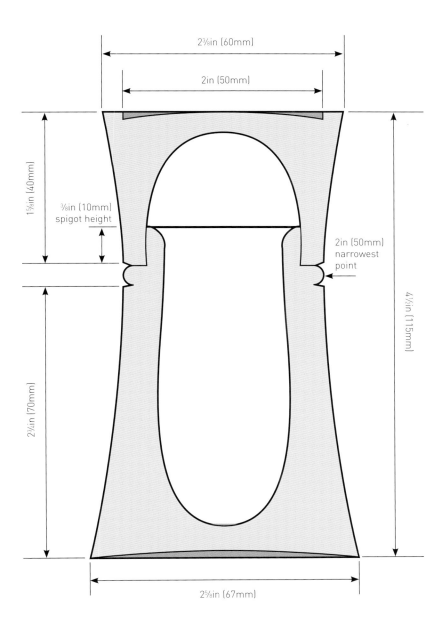

2³⁄₈in (60mm)

2in (50mm)

1⁵⁄₈in (40mm)

³⁄₈in (10mm)
spigot height

2in (50mm)
narrowest
point

4½in (115mm)

2¾in (70mm)

2⁵⁄₈in (67mm)

MAKING THE BOX

The blank I used was already a cylinder, 15in long and 3in in diameter (381mm long and 75mm in diameter). If you have a square blank, make it into a cylinder using the process described for the candlestick (see pages 108–15). Find and mark the centers at each end and fix the blank on the lathe between centers. I held mine between a revolving center and a four-prong drive held in a chuck **1**. Remember to secure the quill lock on the tailstock so the quill cannot come loose during the cutting process. Adjust the rest so that it is about ¼in (6mm) below center and far enough away not to foul

the wood when it is turned by hand. Take a beading and parting tool and cut a tenon on the headstock end to suit your chuck's jaw shape and diameter **2**. Remove the piece from the lathe and secure it in the chuck using the tenon you just cut. Measure and mark a line about 6in (150mm) from the chuck **3**. With a beading and parting tool, cut a tenon at the tailstock end and another on the marked line to suit the chuck jaws. It is best to create a relief or clearance cut to prevent the tool binding in the cut **4**. Remove the waste by making a parting cut in the middle, leaving a

tenon on the piece still held in the headstock. Use a saw to cut the piece through. One section is now in the chuck, and this has a tenon at both ends—one of which is held in the chuck. The other piece can be used for another project some other time **5**. Next, mark what will become the base and the lid sections. Remember the rule of thirds and take into account the spigot join, which is hidden in the lid **6**. Use a beading and parting tool to cut the spigot and a parting tool to cut almost all the way through the box. The tailstock is in place, providing support. Note the little shoulder on the lid

section. This is a reference point showing the diameter of the spigot on which the lid will sit **7**. Remove the lid section and put it to one side. Use a spindle gouge and make the end-grain cut as you did for the end of the candlestick—but you need to go a lot deeper this time. Remember to extract the tool regularly to remove the waste. Take it easy, using successive gentle cuts to cut deeper. You can leave a wall thickness of about $\frac{3}{8}$in (10mm) or more if you are a little worried about making it too thin. In time, as your skill increases, you can make it thinner **8**.

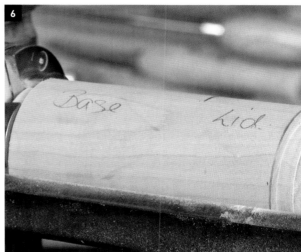

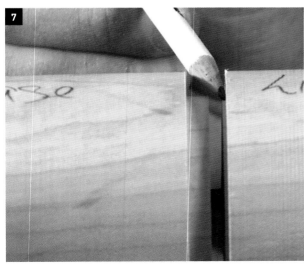

Remember, the flute should point in the direction of the cut. Note the spigot/tenon. We must not make this section too thin so be careful not to swing out the cut too far **9**. After rough shaping the inside with a spindle gouge, clean it up with a French-curve scraper. The cut should occur on or just above the centerline of the work for internal work, but remember the scraper should trail down slightly in use. As with the candlestick, work from the center back out to the top face to ensure you are cutting with the fibers to ensure a clean cut—technically, this is the optimum cutting method used for end-grain work **10**. When you are happy with the shape, you can sand and apply a finish on the inside or do this later on. Next, use a beading and parting tool to make the spigot longer. Do not reduce its diameter; just elongate it so that it measures about ⅜in (10mm) long **11**. Remove the base from the chuck. Now mount the lid in the chuck using the tenon you cut previously. It is prudent to mark the waste section **12**. Use the end-grain cut to remove the bulk. Do not

cut to the full width of what will be the opening indicated by the registration mark left on from the earlier cut **13**, then use a scraper to clean up inside the lid **14**. Use a spindle gouge to undercut the face that meets the shoulder on the base section. This needs to be undercut so that the outer sections of the lid join and the base fit cleanly together **15**. Use a ruler or straight edge to check it is slightly undercut **16**. Check the spigot on the lid section—I used double-ended calipers **17**. Check the lid section using the other end of the calipers **18**. Use a scraper to refine the internal shape and width **19**. Keep checking the fit of base and lid and make adjustments until you have a nicely snug push fit. The reason for using what is called a triple-mount-turning method for this box is to ensure good grain alignment. The only reason the grain may not align perfectly using this method is by taking too large a section out of the middle area to create the spigot—the wider that section, the more risk there is of a grain mismatch **20**.

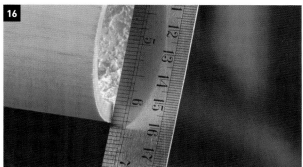

The two faces need to meet together **21**. Remove the corner on the inside, then sand and apply a finish on the inside **22**. Remove the lid and refit the base into the chuck **23**. Use a skew chisel to create an undercut on the spigot shoulder, so that when the lid and base come together they fit neatly on the outer edges of the meeting faces **24**. Here is a tip: Although we have a neat fit in this instance, it may not always be as good. The lid needs to fit and stay put when we turn and refine the top of the lid. If it does not, use kitchen paper to create a tight fit. Don't pack it too tight, or you may split the lid section—use just enough layers of paper to make a tight seal between the lid and the base. Lay the paper over the spigot and slide on the lid; the kitchen paper will form over the spigot. Don't forget, the fit should be secure enough to work on unsupported by the tailstock, but not tight enough to split the wood or not enable you to remove it by hand later on **25**. Use a spindle gouge to clean up the top and to create that top recess detail **26**. Next, move

the rest and use a spindle roughing gouge to shape the outside curve of the box. The lowest part is the join between the lid and the base, but don't go too far or you will cut through to the inside. Use gentle cuts working down toward the join line and do not apply too much pressure onto the wood **27**. Sand and apply a finish to the outside and lid **28**. If you discover any blemishes on the piece do not be afraid to go back and refine the surface, either by sanding or with the gouge. Sand the piece again and finish accordingly. My box

had a light annular ring on the lid, so I skimmed it with a gouge, then sanded and oiled it **29**. To disguise the join, you can cut a bead on the base section using a beading tool. The top edge of the bead will be the point where the lid meets the base **30**. Refine the depth of the bead with a skew chisel. Remember to enter in line with the bevel and only use the lower tip of the tool to cut **31**. When you've finished cutting, sanding, and oiling, remove the lid. The perfectly fitting kitchen paper shows how effective this little trick is **32**.

The base section still needs to be finished off. To do this we are going to make a jamb chuck. Measure the inside opening of the base with calipers **33**. Put an offcut of wood in the chuck—you can use softwood or hardwood—and create a spigot with a slight taper on it, so that the lid will fit tightly while you refine the base. You can fit the box straight onto the wooden jam chuck, but, in doing so, you can bruise the inner surface of the box. To avoid this, you can use the paper-towel method shown earlier when fitting the lid to the jam chuck. Remember the fit must be secure enough

to allow you to cut the work without tailstock support **34**. Bring up the tailstock, centralize, and secure the base **35**. With the tailstock in position, clean up the base so it has a slight undercut. A spindle gouge is ideal for this process. As with the cuts shown previously, the flute points in the direction of cut and the cut occurs on the lower wing of the tool. If you keep the handle low, you can create that shearing cut to minimize grain tearout **36**. When you have gone as far as you can you can, use a thin parting tool to remove most of the stub of wood under the revolving center

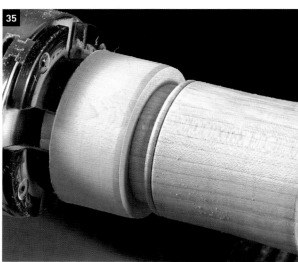

then remove the tailstock **37**. Stop the lathe, remove the tailstock and check the work is secure. Restart the lathe and clean up the remainder of the base with a spindle gouge, then use a beading and parting tool to create a series of grooves on the bottom. This is a gentle push cut and only the corner of beading and parting tool is used for this. It is a small detail, but it is pleasing to see **38**. The areas that are not usually seen should be finished to the same standard as all other parts. Sand and oil the bottom. Then remove the section from the lathe and fit the two parts together. Hopefully the fit is still good—not so tight that it won't come off, but not too tight that one has to pull heavily on the two parts to cause them to separate **39**. The final result should be a box that feels and looks good and is smooth to the touch both inside and out **40**. Boxes can be made to any shape and size. We use larger ones to store rice and pasta, but they can also be of a size to be just big enough to hold a single ring or your pills/medication. Boxes are great fun to make so experiment with different shapes and offcuts of wood to find out what you like. Just remember to work safely and have fun.

FURTHER READING

Darlow, Mike, *Woodturning Methods*, ISBN 978-1-56523-372-0

Darlow, Mike, *Fundamentals of Woodturning*, ISBN 978-1-56523-355-3

Hayes, Derek, *Woodturning Design*, ISBN 978-1-86108-865-9

Holtham, Alan, *Woodturning Spindle Projects*, ISBN 978-1-86108-642-6

O'Donnell, Michael, *Woodturning Techniques*, ISBN 978-1-86108-283-1

Raffan, Richard, *The Art of Turned Bowls*, ISBN 978-1-56158-954-8

Raffan, Richard, *The New Turning Wood with Richard Raffan*, ISBN 978-1-56158-957-9

Raffan, Richard, *The Complete Illustrated Guide to Turning*, ISBN 978-1-56158-672-1

Raffan, Richard, *Turning Projects*, ISBN 978-0-94239-138-1

Raffan, Richard *Turning Boxes with Richard Raffan*, ISBN 978-1-56158-509-0

Rowley, Keith, *Woodturning: A Foundation Course*, ISBN 978-1-86108-114-8

Stott, Chris, *Turned Boxes 50 Designs*, ISBN 978-1-86108-203-9

ACKNOWLEDGMENTS

Special thanks for assistance during the shooting and creation of this book go to:

Ashley Iles (Edge Tools) Ltd
Tel: +44 (0)1790 763372
www.ashleyiles.turningtools.co.uk

Craft Supplies USA
Tel: 1 800 551 8876
www.woodturnerscatalog.com

Crown Hand Tools Ltd
Tel: +44 (0)1142 612300
www.crownhandtools.ltd.uk

Henry Taylor Tools Ltd
Tel: +44 (0)1142 340282
www.henrytaylortools.co.uk

Robert Sorby
Tel: +44 (0)1142 250700
www.robert-sorby.co.uk

Woodcraft, North Clearwater, Florida
Tel: 727 532 6888
clearwater@mywoodcraft.com

Thanks also to: **Alan Goodsell, Aaron Shedlock, Virginia Brehaut, Walter Hall,** and **Chris West**

INDEX

To request a full catalog of GMC titles, please contact:

GMC Publications Ltd
Castle Place, 166 High Street, Lewes,
East Sussex, BN7 1XU, United Kingdom

Tel: +44 (0)1273 488005
Fax: +44 (0)1273 402866
www.thegmcgroup.com